Exposing Myths Heard in Church

By Dell Young

Revealing God's Grace through Jesus Christ

ISBN 13: 978-1-946629-20-3
ISBN 10: 1-946629-20-0

www.dellyoung.net

Dedication

I dedicate this book to my wonderful wife Jill and our three amazing children, Justin, Kristin, and Austin. Their faithful love and support has given me the courage to write this book. I also dedicate this book as part of my legacy to my precious grandchildren, Lakelyn, Ayden, Addyson, and Abel. Poppy loves each of you.

Contents

Preface

I realize that by writing this book I am challenging some things that most of us grew up hearing preached in church. Many things that we have long held as truth are simply myths and are not found in the Bible. I had been taught by the church that three wise men visited baby Jesus the night He was born and laid in a Bethlehem manger. However, as I read the Bible for myself, I discovered that this was not true. Would it surprise you then that not even a single wise man ever made it to the manger scene the night Jesus was born? The fact is the Bible clearly says they came to the house (not manger) where the young Child (not babe) was and worshipped Him. Yes, it's stunning, but true nonetheless.

The Bible commanded the parents of a first-born male child to bring a lamb to the priest as a burnt offering (Leviticus, Chapter 12), but if they could not afford a lamb, then they could bring a young pigeon or a turtledove as a sin offering. Joseph and Mary brought the offering of the poor. Per scripture, this offering was to be brought thirty-three days after the male child was born.

> [22] *Now when the days of her purification according to the law of Moses were completed, they brought Him to Jerusalem to present Him to the Lord* [23] *(as it is written in the law of the Lord, "Every male who opens the womb shall be called holy to the LORD"),* [24] *and to offer a sacrifice according to what is said in the law of the Lord, "A pair of turtledoves or two young pigeons."* (Luke 2:22-24 NKJV)[1]

To believe that Joseph and Mary were given gold, frankincense, and myrrh the night Jesus was born, and yet thirty-three days later they refused to spend any of it to obey the law of God and buy a lamb is to believe they were liars and cheaters. It says that they were too cheap to use any of those valuable gifts to buy a lamb for sacrifice and, therefore, brought the offering of the poor. Their offering of a pigeon or a turtledove a month after Jesus' birth proves that they were poor. This proves that the wise men had not yet visited them and given them these very valuable and costly gifts.

If people would just read their Bibles, they'd realize that what they've been told all these years is simply not what happened. There's much proof in the Bible that this myth is not true. Yet millions of people and most of the church are under the impression that such a birthday scenario is recorded in the Bible, and it's been reproduced in countless church plays, movies, television specials, and Christmas cards.

Some of you may be thinking, "What does it matter?" You might think that I'm making too much of this. It matters because

---

1 All verses are from the NKJV unless otherwise noted.

it's not true! It matters because the Bible matters. If we could get the birth of Jesus this wrong, I wonder what else we have wrong. What other things have been preached to us that are simply myths?

I mean no disrespect in exposing these myths that I address in this book. I, in the past, taught many of these myths as truth until I came to know the revelation of God's Amazing Grace. Today in the church, we need a theological reformation that will liberate believers to break free from the bondage of performance-based religion and into life-giving grace.

Introduction

Ephesians 5:8-11

For you were once darkness, but now you are light in the Lord.
Walk as children of light (for the fruit of the Spirit is in all goodness,
righteousness, and truth), finding out what is acceptable to the Lord.
And have no fellowship with the unfruitful works of darkness, but
rather expose them.

My purpose in writing this book is to expose the myths that
have been heard in church and to help believers to break free from
the bondage of religion that has been placed on them by people
who had good intentions, but who only taught the religious
doctrines and traditions that they themselves were taught. I was
told that once you submit a manuscript to a publisher, one of the
first questions they ask is, "What qualifies you to write this book?"
My qualifications come out of my own experience with legalistic
religion. I was taught from my childhood that my salvation was
based upon my confession of my sins and that I would have to

maintain my salvation by being sure to confess and repent of every sin that I committed. I remember how frightened I became after hearing a sermon in which the preacher said, "No sin will ever enter into heaven." The implication (as I understood it) was that if I died with some unconfessed sin in my life, I would go straight to hell. So, I struggled with this thought for many years, that the odds of me making it to heaven were not good. I remember often being tempted to just give up and go back to my old sinful life, knowing that I probably would not make it anyway.

It would be many years later before the revelation of God's Amazing Grace came into my life. When I finally saw that my salvation rested solely upon God's covenant oath and His Work within me, that He made Him who knew no sin *to be* sin for me, that I could become the righteousness of God in Christ, this truth radically set me free. A tremendous burden was lifted off me. No longer was I sin conscious, but I became Christ conscious. I no longer depended upon my obedience, but now I focused on His Obedience. My faith was now totally in the Grace of God.

I admit that in the past I have taught most of these myths that I will cover in this book. As far as my preaching, I was for the most part a product of my surroundings. I simply repeated the same doctrinal positions I grew up hearing in church. I had been taught very well that *"we all have sinned and fall short of the glory of God"* (Romans 3:23), but no one had taught me the next verse, that *"being justified (made righteous) freely by His grace through the redemption that is in Christ Jesus."* I didn't know that His Righteousness was a gift to me. The issue is not that you sin, because you will sin. The issue is what you believe when you sin.

Do You Believe:

- That when you are going through difficult times that maybe you're being punished for your past sins, that you're reaping what you sowed years ago as a sinner, that maybe your sins have come home to roost?

- Do you believe in generational curses?

- Do you feel like you are not pleasing to God?

- Do you feel God is disappointed with you when you sin, that He is angry with you?

- When you sin, do you want to run to God or hide from Him?

- Do you believe that as a believer when you sin that you are no longer righteous and that you have fallen from grace?

- Do you believe that when you sin that you are out of fellowship with God and that you must "DO" something to get back right with God?

- Do you pray prayers like: "Lord, please give me your favor; Lord, please hear my prayer? Lord, please bless me; Lord, please be with me today?" Do you pray for an open heaven? Do you pray for the mind of Christ? Do you ask God for more of Him?

- Do you believe that even though you're born again that you're still a sinner and not a saint?

This book will help answer these questions and many more. This book will boldly proclaim the message of God's grace, forgiveness, and unconditional love. My prayer is that you will be set free from the confusing mixture of Law and grace, the very thing Jesus died to set us free from. Jesus said:

> *No one puts a piece from a new garment on an old one, otherwise the new makes a tear, and also the piece that was taken out of the new does not match the old. And no one puts new wine into old wineskins; or else the new wine will burst the wineskins and be spilled, and the wineskins will be ruined. But new wine must be put into new wineskins, and both are preserved. And no one, having drunk old wine, immediately desires new; for he says, "The old is better".* (Luke 5:37-39)

The natural man likes his old ways. He likes his old wine – that is, his old religion. It's important to recognize that Jesus brought something new to mankind – the gospel. Grace and truth. He did not come into the world to do any patching on the old garment. He did not come to patch up the Law. He came to fulfill it and to pay the penalty of sin by dying on the cross. He brought us the new wine of the gospel. This new wine must be placed into the new wineskin of grace, not into the old wineskin of the law. He came to give us something new.

There is an old way that leads to frustration and disappointment. There is a new and living way (Hebrews 10:20) that comes free of your efforts and works. It is a gift that changes everything. There also is a third way – a hybrid, or a mix, of the Old and the New – that you find in most churches today.

A hybrid is a mixture of two different things. There are hybrid cars. They have both a gas and an electric motor. A mule is a hybrid of a donkey and a horse. Although Jesus warned us about this mixture of the new with the old, much of the church continues to teach a mix of the Old Covenant and the New Covenant. They preach you are saved by grace, and then teach that your salvation is kept only by you confessing each sin as you commit it. In other words, that you are saved by grace but kept by law. This is more than just mixing a little Old with New. It's a whole new breed of religion. It is like a mule. It's not a donkey, nor is it a horse.

The pure undiluted gospel of grace sounds too good to be true; therefore, they have mixed some of the old and new together and produced a gospel that Apostle Paul says is no gospel at all. (Galatians 1:6-7)

This hybrid message says we must obey some of the laws of the Old, especially the Ten Commandments. God wants us to be able to rightly divide the Word and clearly separate what belongs to the Old Covenant of Law and what belongs to the New Covenant of grace. Many believers today are living as if the cross did not make any difference! Those who preach this hybrid tell us that we must confess each of our sins as we crawl to the throne of grace. If we fail to confess one of our sins, then we're not forgiven, and if the rapture occurs, then you will surely be left behind. And that God is displeased with us, even angry, and that we are out of fellowship with God until we get ourselves back into fellowship by repenting. That we need to put our sins under the blood of Jesus, as if His Blood didn't pay for and remove every sin. How ridiculous!

There are huge differences in the Old Covenant and the New Covenant regarding how sin is dealt with. In the Old Covenant, people were forgiven for their sins by atonement. Their sin was not removed, but the sin was covered. In the New Covenant, Jesus took away the sin of the whole world! (John 1:29)

God's grace is not one subject of the Bible. Grace is THE subject of the Bible. Grace is a Person, and His name is Jesus. Jesus did not come to preach grace, but to be grace. To be saved by grace is to be saved by Him. I have watched this revelation of God's grace bring people into a passionate, powerful, and liberating relationship with their heavenly Father. I can never go back to trying to relate to God under the mixed message of law and grace.

Reading this book could cause you to experience a newfound identity, freedom, and boldness. I believe this book will cause you to go back and take a second look at some of the things that you've heard preached in church and to ask yourself if those viewpoints are biblical truths or religious myths.

Chapter 1

Myth: God Is in Control

This is a phrase that I hear used often, mostly when something goes wrong. "God is in control," it is said when someone dies, when a devastating storm hits, when our health fails.

One of the biggest areas of confusion in the church is in the sovereignty of God. We know that God is all-powerful and all-knowing; therefore, we assume He is in control of everything that happens here on earth. I don't know of any teaching that has done more to impugn the name of God than the teaching that God is in control of everything that happens on earth. I've heard things like this all my life:

"I got cancer, but God allowed this to happen. He's trying to teach me something."

"God took my child. I guess He needed another angel in Heaven."

"God allowed this evil in my life. He has a purpose for it somehow."

Statements like this are not only ignorant, but also blasphemous. How many people did Jesus give a disease to when He walked the earth? How many storms did He send or bless? Show me one person that came to Jesus for healing that He sent away still sick. Jesus did none of these things, yet some Christians believe that His Father does them or "allows" them on a regular basis.

In fact, the Bible never says God is in control, but it does say that the devil has control:

> *We know that we are children of God, and that the whole world is under the control of the evil one.* (1 John 5:19 NIV)

The NKJV says, "under the sway of the wicked one." Much of the world is under the influence of evil. Satan was defeated at the cross, but he still has sway or control wherever the gospel is not believed and people yield to him.

God does not control us. He does not give us a free will and then take it away. If God were truly in control, there would be no murders, no rapes, no sickness. Not everything that happens is God's will. If everything that ever happened on earth was God's will, there would be no reason to pray, *"Thy will be done on earth as it is in heaven"* (Matthew 6:10). Much of what we see here is not God's will. Saying that God is in control is not only biblically wrong, but using this phrase can also be dangerous. It causes people to blame God and shun taking responsibility for their own actions. Why?

Because *the heaven, even the heavens, are the LORD'S; But the earth He has given to the children of men* (Psalm 115:16).

God desires His Will to be done on earth as it is in Heaven. God's will is that not any should perish, yet people perish every day. God's will is for all men to repent, yet most don't. Why did Jesus ever raise anyone from the dead when He walked the earth? Some believe that when people die (regardless of their age or the cause) it was just their "time to go." This is what you hear in church at funerals. They say things like "God never makes a mistake," so you're not to question the death. Jesus went about healing the sick and even raising the dead. If their deaths were "God's will," then Jesus was working against the will of His Father by raising them from the dead. If God were making people sick, or "allowing them to be sick," then Jesus was working against the will of His Father by healing them, and the Father and Son are a house divided. God is in charge, but He is not in control. Think about it like this: the police department is in charge of your city to prevent crimes and protect citizens, but they are not in control. If the police were truly in control of the city, there would be no rapes or murders in that city. If God were in control of everything, then He would be responsible for all the evil in our world – all the wars, killings, disease, and destruction. But God is not the author of evil. In Him, there is no shadow at all.

Is every leader over us God's choice? I hear preachers preaching that every leader/king is God's choice and God's will. They quote Daniel 2:21 as proof. This is not a proof text that God chooses every leader here on earth. Daniel is blessing God for revealing to him the interpretation of Nebuchadnezzar's dream. The Bible is clear that wicked people become leaders/kings. Is this God's will? Does He place the wicked in power?

> [2] *When the righteous are in authority, the people rejoice; But when a wicked man rules, the people groan.* (Proverbs 29:2)

Pastor Bill Johnson says, "Any definition of God's sovereignty that allows evil to exist as a part of His Will and purpose is an IMMORAL definition of sovereignty." If you believe God chooses every leader, then you must believe God chose Hitler. You can't have it both ways. The problem with thinking "God is in control" is it makes us passive spectators in the ride of life. I have seen so many Christians not vote because of this teaching that God chooses our president, that God raises up one leader and removes another. So, they just stay home and say, "What's the use for me to vote? God will place in office who He wants. We'll just sit here and take whatever life hands us saying, 'Whatever will be will be'."

The truth is that God is not in control of everything. He has given us His Authority to resist the devil and his evil influence. We have been empowered to be light, salt, to heal the sick, cast out demons, to reveal the gospel of His Grace in dark places. Not everything that happens is God's will. Consider:

- It was not God's will for Adam to eat from the forbidden tree (Genesis 2:17), but Adam ate.

- God is not willing that any perish (2 Peter 3:9), yet people perish.

- God commands all people everywhere to repent (Acts 17:30), yet many don't.

This is God's gift to us – the freedom to choose how we live. The problem is we often make choices contrary to God's will. We are free to decide how we spend our money, who we elect as president, how we drive our cars, who we marry, what career path we should follow. So herein lies the thorny theological paradox. How does God's sovereignty and human free will interact?

Why do you think Jesus taught us to pray, "Let your will be done on earth as it is in heaven"?

The "God is sovereign" statement is spoken nearly every time something bad happens, but it's just not true. The word "sovereign" is not even in the Bible!

Sovereignty of God

Many believe the Lord causes all their problems. They have resigned themselves to the "sovereignty of God." I believe this is possibly the worst doctrine in the church. The way the sovereignty of God is taught today is one of the devil's biggest inroads into our lives. If this belief is true, then our actions are irrelevant, our efforts are meaningless, and our prayers are useless.

The word "sovereign" is not used in the KJV or the NKJV of the Bible. It is used 303 times in the Old Testament of the *New International Version,* but it is always used in association with the word "LORD" and is the equivalent of the *King James Version's* "LORD God." Not even one of those times is the word "sovereign" used in the manner that it has come to be used in religion in our day. Religion has invented a new meaning for the word "sovereign" that basically means God controls everything. Nothing can happen but what He wills or allows. However, there is nothing in the actual definition that states that. The dictionary defines "sovereign" as:

1. Paramount; supreme. 2. Having supreme rank or power. 3. Independent: a sovereign state. 4. Excellent.

None of these definitions means that God controls everything.

It is assumed that since God is paramount or supreme that nothing can happen without His Approval. Typical teaching on the sovereignty of God puts Jesus in the driver's seat with us as passengers. The truth is we are the ones steering the car of our own lives. We are the one doing the driving. If Jesus was driving, then our lives would never be wrecked. We are supposed to take directions from the Lord, but He doesn't do the driving for us.

Man has been given the authority over his own life, but he must have the Holy Spirit leading him to succeed. The Holy Spirit leads and guides us into the truth that sets us free. A guide is just that – a guide – not a drill sergeant. John explains this in John 16:13. The Holy Spirit wants to direct our steps. God created us to be dependent upon Him, and our independence is at the root of all our problems.

James 4:7 says, *"Submit yourselves therefore to God. Resist the devil, and he will flee from you."*

This verse makes it clear that some things are from God, and some things are from the devil. We are to submit to the things that are from God and resist the things that are from the devil. The word "resist" means to stand against. Saying "whatever will be, will be" is not standing against the devil. If a person truly believed that God is the one who put sickness on them because He is trying to teach them something, then they should not go to the doctor or take any medicine. They should let the sickness run its course and thereby get the full benefit of God's teachings. That is ridiculous.

It is even more ridiculous to believe that God is the one behind the sickness or problem.

Acts 10:38 says that Jesus *"healed all those who were oppressed OF THE DEVIL."* It was not God who oppressed them with sickness. It was the devil. It's the same today. Sickness is from the devil, not from God. We need to resist sickness and, by faith, submit ourselves to healing, which is from God by the stripes of Jesus Christ.

It's normally at this point that someone says, "What about Job?" My quick answer is that I'm not a disciple of Job. I'm a disciple of Jesus. Job was the question; Jesus is the answer. Job had an inferior revelation of God. Job said that he had spoken things that he didn't understand or know.

> *You asked, "Who is this who hides counsel without knowledge?" Therefore I have uttered what I did not understand, Things too wonderful for me, which I did not know.* (Job 42:3)

> *⁵I have heard of You by the hearing of the ear, But now my eye sees You. ⁶ Therefore I abhor myself, And repent in dust and ashes.* (Job 42:5-6)

What if the only Bible verses about Jesus were Him making a whip and driving the money changers out of the temple? (See John 2:15) Would that be wrong? NO, just incomplete. We must remember Job wasn't born again. He didn't have a Bible. He had an incomplete revelation about God. He didn't see God as Father. Jesus came to show us the Father.

> *³ who being the brightness of His glory and the express image of His person, and upholding all things by the word of His power, when*

He had by Himself purged our sins, sat down at the right hand of the Majesty on high (Hebrews 1:3)

The NIV says that Jesus is *"the radiance of God's glory and the exact representation of his being"* (Hebrews 1:3) If we want to see the Father, then we must look at Jesus (John 14:9). Many have some messed up notions about God because they fail to look at Jesus. Our concept of God must come from the person of Jesus Christ. The way many believers approach their concept of God is to convey that they do not need the revelation of God that came through Jesus.

You should call into question anything that you think you know about God that you can't see in Jesus. Jesus Christ is perfect theology.

For some strange reason, people seem to find comfort in believing that God is responsible for their loss or suffering. In the New Testament, Jesus bore our curse for us (Galatians 3:13). The Lord would no more put sickness on a New Testament believer than He would cause us to sin. The revelation that God is not the author of my sickness, sin, or pain has changed my view of Him more than anything else. Any problems, pains, or sicknesses in my life are not from God, but from the devil. They are a result of my own decisions or just the results of life on a fallen planet.

Every good gift and every perfect gift is from above, and comes down from the Father of lights, with whom there is no variation or shadow of turning. (James 1:17)

My theology has become rather simple: God good, devil bad. If it is good, it is from God. If it's bad, it's not from my Father. Maybe you came to God because of something bad or painful in your life that overwhelmed you and caused you to turn to Him for help. That pain or circumstance, even though because of it you came to the Lord, was not from Him, regardless of the outcome. It was your faith that you placed in His Grace that turned your life around, not the problem.

Terrorist actions or shootings happen, and God doesn't stop them. A tornado flattens a town, and the insurance companies call it "an act of God." When something bad happens, we blame our government, our parents, our spouses, and our kids. We blame the system, the "man", the immigrants, the Communists, and, most of all, we blame God. The blame game started in the garden with Adam and Eve, and it has not stopped. Adam essentially blamed God for his fall. He said in Genesis 3:12:

> *Then the man said, "The woman whom You gave to be with me, she gave me of the tree, and I ate."*

The woman blamed the serpent. We have been blaming one another ever since the beginning. Everything that happens is because God gave us the freedom to do what we like, even the freedom to hate Him, kill our brothers, and then blame Him for what we did. Jesus, on the other hand, never blamed anyone. He who knew no sin became sin for us. He fixed our mess.

Read in The Message Bible John 9:2-3:

> [2] *His disciples asked, "Rabbi, who sinned: this man or his parents, causing him to be born blind?" [3] Jesus said, "You're asking the wrong question. You're looking for someone to blame. There is no such cause-effect here. Look instead for what God can do."*

Stop trying to blame someone for the problem, and instead look to God for the answer!

God is not the one making you sick, depressed, sad, or poor! He did not cause your marriage to fail, your kids to rebel, or your company to fire you. This is not Heaven. We live on a fallen planet, but God through His Grace has provided everything that we would ever need through the Cross of Jesus Christ.

> ³ *as His divine power has given to us all things that pertain to life and godliness, through the knowledge of Him who called us by glory and virtue.* (2 Peter 1:3)

He HAS given to us all things that pertain to life and godliness. We have been given His Divine Power to overcome.

I pray that we stop saying, "God is in control" and start saying "God is always good. My life is filled with choices, and my choices have consequences. If pain occurs, it is not my Father's will. A life consecrated to God means that no matter what happens to me that is outside God's will for my life, He can make all things work together for good to those who love him."

Chapter 2

Myth: Christians Are Just Sinners Saved by Grace

It is a myth that even after you've been born again you are just a sinner who has been saved by grace. We are not sinners, but we are not saints! Notice that almost all the epistles in the New Testament are addressed to the saints, not to you sinners. This lie has caused many to live a life of constant defeat and despair, far from the overcoming and victorious life promised us in the Bible. If I was still a sinner after the new birth, then what was accomplished?

Therefore, if anyone is in Christ, he is a new creation; old things have passed away; behold, all things have become new. (2 Corinthians 5:17)

To insist on still calling yourself a sinner diminishes the value of the finished work of Jesus on the cross. Indeed, to still call myself essentially a sinner dishonours the amazing grace of the gospel. The Greek word which we translate "gospel" literally means nearly-too-good-to-be-true news. If I insist on saying that Christians are still sinners, what is the Good News? We have an identity crisis in the body of Christ. We know what we were, but we need a revelation of what we are in Christ Jesus. Paul provides a horrible list of the evils that had formerly characterized the believers at Corinth, such as fornicators, idolaters, adulterers, thieves, drunkards and so on. But he clearly adds, *"**Such WERE some of you,** but you were washed but you were sanctified, but you were justified in the name of our Lord Jesus Christ and the Spirit of our God"* (1 Corinthians 6:16). Surely, he is telling them (and us) that they are now saints of God, set apart.

Most Christians find it almost impossible to call themselves saints. Why? Because we still sin. They don't understand that the term "saint" is your identity, not necessarily your behaviour. Unfortunately, in this age of conflict with the world, the flesh, and the devil, we still sin, but when we sin now, we sin as a saint. The word "saint" in the Bible means "an awesome thing, blameless, holy, pure, clean, perfect." We recoil from this description of ourselves. This sounds like the epitome of arrogance and pride, but this is precisely what the Bible calls those in Christ.

We readily accept that the world is full of sinners, but most Christians are confused as to why they were sinners in the first place. They think they're called sinners because they sinned. Suppose I ask you, "How many sins do you have to commit to be a sinner?" Most of you would answer "one." However, that's incorrect. The answer is none! You were not a sinner because you sinned. You sinned because you were a sinner. It is extremely important that you realize that you were born a sinner. You have no choice but to sin, that's what sinners do, they sin.

> *For as by one man's disobedience **many were made sinners,** so also by one Man's obedience **many will be made righteous.** (Romans 5:19)*

We're born sinners. If we believe that we became a sinner because we committed a sin, then we presume that doing precedes being. Therefore, people become sinners or saints by doing. We are not "human-doings", but human beings. If we can grasp that we're sinners by birth, then we can see how by the new birth alone we become saints.

I've heard Christians make this statement in conversation, "I'm not trying to be a saint or anything but ..." and then they finish their comments. This is the problem, we don't see ourselves as righteous; therefore, we don't see ourselves as saints. You may be thinking, "What's the big deal? Why do I need to know I'm a saint?" Because the Bible says, "As he thinks in his heart, so is he" (Proverbs 23:7). A person will not behave in ways that are contrary to what they believe about themselves. If you believe that at your core you are still a sinner, then sinning will be normal for you.

> *and that you put on the new man which **was created** according to God, in true righteousness and holiness.* (Ephesians 4:24)

"WAS CREATED" THAT WAY! "Was" is past tense. Your new spirit was created in true righteousness and true holiness. It is not a process of becoming that way. You were born again that way.

When you were born again, your spirit that was dead has now been made alive in Christ (Colossians 2:13).

I think many Christians still see themselves as sinners because they believe God sees them that way. They think that God just calls us righteous even though He knows we are not really righteous. I hear Christians say, "We are righteous in His Eyes." (I will deal with this in the next chapter). They see God as if HE's wearing a pair of Jesus glasses that hide our true condition from His view, that God is just pretending that we are righteous. God calls us righteous because we actually are righteous.

But he who is joined to the Lord is one spirit with Him. (1 Corinthians 6:17)

Have you been joined to the Lord? Are you saying that Christ has been united with sin? If we don't claim we're saints, or that we're righteous, then we're saying something different than God says. We're lowering God's standard, and we insult the work of Jesus on the cross. The New Testament calls you a saint sixty-three times! Stop calling yourself a sinner saved by grace. It's a lie. When you know the truth about your identity in Christ, you are free to live the life of victory that is your right by the new birth.

Chapter 3

Myth: We Are Righteous in God's Sight

Upon first reading this statement, you may be thinking, "Where is the myth?" If the statement was, "We are righteous," then that is true, but it's when we add "in God's sight" that causes the problem. As I said in the previous chapter, some think that God just calls us righteous even though He knows we are not really righteous. God is not just pretending that we are righteous. God calls us righteous because we have been made righteous.

> *For He made Him who knew no sin to be sin for us, that we might become the righteousness of God in Him.* (2 Corinthians 5:21)

This verse is absolutely clear. Jesus took our sin so we could have His Righteousness. Jesus was made sin with my sin, so that I could be made righteous with His Righteousness. Jesus had no sin of His Own, just as I had no righteousness of my own. Jesus was made sin without sinning, that I could be made righteous without my works. The righteousness that we have is the very righteousness of Jesus Christ, a righteousness that has never known sin!

> *For as by one man's disobedience many were made sinners, so also by one Man's obedience many will be made righteous.* (Romans 5:19)

We were made sinners not by our personal sin. Therefore, we're made righteous not by our personal righteous deeds. One man (Adam) made you a sinner. Therefore, one Man (Christ) makes you righteous. Adam's disobedience (not mine) made me a sinner. Therefore, Christ's obedience (not mine) makes me and keeps me righteous. If MY sin made me a sinner, then my righteousness must make me righteous. One man got me in this mess, so one Man can get me out. I got in this by natural birth. I get out of it by being born again by supernatural birth. It is His Obedience and His Righteousness that brings me out!

> *For in it the righteousness of God is revealed from faith to faith; as it is written, "The just shall live by faith."* (Romans 1:17)

> *For if by the one man's offense death reigned through the one, much more those who receive abundance of grace and of the gift of righteousness will reign in life through the One, Jesus Christ.* (Romans 5:17)

Notice that righteousness is revealed and that righteousness is a gift. It is the righteousness of God that is revealed and not the sinfulness of man. Righteousness is received, not achieved. It is a gift, not a paycheck. There is nothing more important for you than to get the revelation of the righteousness of God by faith.

There is blessing, power, and peace that come with the righteousness of God. Righteousness is the main theme of scripture. If you're not righteous, you're unrighteous. There is no in-between. It's like being pregnant. Either you are or you're not! You're not a "little bit pregnant," nor are you a little righteous. All of God's promises and blessings are to and for the righteous. He has nothing to offer the unrighteous. Heaven is made for the righteous. Read how the Bible speaks of the righteous:

The righteous are bold as a lion. (Proverbs 28:1)

The prayers of a righteous man avails much. (James 5:16)

The righteous run into the Lord as their Hightower and are saved. (Proverb 18:10)

The eyes of the Lord are upon the righteous, His ears open to their cry. (Psalm 34:15)

DAVID said: I have never seen the righteous forsaken or his seed begging bread. (Psalm 37:25)

Many are the afflictions of the righteous, but the Lord delivers him out of them all. (Psalm 34:19)

He shall never permit the righteous to be moved. (Psalm 55:22)

A righteous man may fall seven times, but he rises back up. (Proverbs 24:16)

I hear well-meaning preachers teach about a "positional righteous." They say that righteousness is our position in Christ, but we are not actually righteous. I would ask this question, "Does the Bible say that Jesus just positionally took our sin or does it say He made Him to BE sin for us?" The thought that He literally became sin so that we could become positionally righteous is ridiculous. I understand how they could arrive at this if they look at the outward man and not at the man within. Were we positionally made sinners by Adam's disobedience, or were we literal sinners? Since we were made literal sinners by Adam's sin, we are made literally righteous by Christ's righteousness.

> *For with the heart one believes unto righteousness, and with the mouth confession is made unto salvation.* (Romans 10:10)

You believe you are righteous in your heart. You need to confess that you are righteous, especially when you have sinned. You may not feel righteous, but you still are righteous.

Remember your righteousness is not your own. It's a gift. A gift can't be earned. If you didn't earn it by your deeds, you can't un-earn it by your sin. Your righteousness is an everlasting righteousness (Psalm 119:142). If when you sin, you lose your righteousness, then your sin is stronger than Jesus' righteousness. I'm not saying sin doesn't matter. I'm not making little of sin. I'm making much of Jesus! You will be persecuted (mostly by the church) for believing that you are righteous no matter what you've done.

> *Blessed are those who are persecuted for righteousness' sake, For theirs is the kingdom of heaven.* (Matthew 5:10)

One of the main reasons why many Christians suffer from condemnation, fear, and depression is they refuse to wear the *breastplate of righteousness* (Ephesians 6:14). God's righteousness covers your heart and emotions. Satan is an accuser. It is one of his greatest weapons.

You are no good.

You are a terrible husband.

You are a pathetic mother.

Christians that don't believe they are truly righteous just accept this condemnation. We put on His Righteousness. It is His Breastplate that protects us. It has nothing to do with your performance. All your righteousness is filthy rags. It won't cover you, protect you, or comfort you. You will have days when you fail, when you sin. That's when you must remind yourself (and satan) that all your sin was imputed to Him, and all His Righteousness was imputed to you. His Purity, His Righteousness, and His Pleasing the Father have all been accredited to me as though I did it! We are righteous as a gift! It is not the breastplate of performance! Jesus' righteousness is a breastplate that never changes, never wears out, and is spotless.

Don't believe the myth that you are not truly righteous. Jesus has given us His Righteousness. It won't do you any good if you don't believe it. Live your life out of this great revelation, and this truth will radically transform and empower your life.

Chapter 4

Myth: Our Sins Are Under the Blood of Jesus

This myth is repeated often in church. Sometimes it is said from one believer to another, "You just need to put that sin under the blood." Or we are assured by the speaker that our sins are under the blood of Jesus. You may be thinking "Well, aren't they?" NO! Jesus Christ did not come to merely cover our sins. He came to remove sin.

> *The next day John saw Jesus coming toward him, and said, "Behold! The Lamb of God who **takes away the sin of the world**!* (John 1:29)

*And He Himself is the propitiation for our sins, and not for ours only but also **for the whole world.*** (1 John 2:2)

*For it is not possible that the blood of bulls and goats could **take away sins.*** (Hebrews 10:4)

It is clear from these scriptures that Jesus took away the sin of the world. Did Jesus accomplish His Mission? Did His Sacrifice take away the sin of the world or not? Under the Old Covenant, sin was "covered" or atoned for. Atonement is the Hebrew word "Kapar" which means to cover. The blood of innocent animals offered for men's sins under the Old Covenant did not remove their sin, but covered their sins. Their sins were pushed forward, but never taken away.

[11] And every priest stands ministering daily and offering repeatedly the same sacrifices, which can never take away sins. [12] But this Man, after He had offered one sacrifice for sins forever, sat down at the right hand of God, (Hebrews 10:11-12)

Jesus came to do something that no Levitical Priest could ever do. After offering Himself as a sacrifice on the cross, He sat down. He didn't sit down because He was tired. He sat down because "it is finished!" The Old Covenant priest "stands daily and offering repeatedly." They never sat down because their work was never finished. Jesus offered one sacrifice, a better sacrifice (Hebrews 9:23), that took away sin. The Law and the old sacrificial system was just a shadow of good things to come:

[1] For the law, having a shadow of the good things to come, and not the very image of the things, can never with these same sacrifices, which they offer continually year by year, make those who approach perfect. [2] For then would they not have ceased to be offered? For the

worshipers, once purified, would have had no more consciousness of sins. ³ But in those sacrifices there is a reminder of sins every year. (Hebrews 10:1-3)

Jesus Christ was the Good that was to come! He didn't come to hide our sins from God's eyes, but to remove them as far as the east is from the west (Psalm 103:12). Jesus removed our "consciousness of sins" because His Blood purified us, made us righteous. Under the old sacrificial system, there is a reminder of sins every year. Today most believers are reminded of their sins daily by satan and weekly by the church. (I will deal with this in detail in the next chapter.). It may sound like a good thing for someone to tell you that your sins are under the blood, but it is a myth. This myth minimizes the work of Jesus and the power of His Blood to remove sin. God is not relating to you based on your sin, but on the basis of His Son. Why? Because your sin does not exist. His Blood removed it.

Chapter 5

Myth: We Need to Be More Sin Conscious

¹ For the law, having a shadow of the good things to come, and not the very image of the things, can never with these same sacrifices, which they offer continually year by year, make those who approach perfect. ² For then would they not have ceased to be offered? For the worshipers, once purified, would have had no more consciousness of sins. ³ But in those sacrifices there is a reminder of sins every year. ⁴ For it is not possible that the blood of bulls and goats could take away sins. (Hebrews 10:1-4)

Hebrews points out that the old sacrifices didn't work. If they had, two things would have happened. First, they would have stopped offering them, and secondly, if they worked, the people would no longer have had a consciousness of sin. They would have stopped focusing on sin. Trying to overcome sin by focusing on sin is like trying to overcome eating sweets by staring at a chocolate cake. There is only one action that results in forgiveness and cleansing of sin – blood sacrifice.

> *And according to the law almost all things are purified with blood, and without shedding of blood there is no remission.* (Hebrews 9:22)

If we accept the fact that God's only economy for the forgiveness of sin is the shedding of blood, then this will radically change our view on how we stand before God. No amount of talking to God about your sin, no amount of crying, begging, or asking God to forgive us will bring cleansing and forgiveness in our lives. We've heard it sung in church, "Nothing but the blood of Jesus," yet most of the church believes it is the blood of Jesus PLUS our confession that brings forgiveness.

The shedding of blood is the one and only action that results in forgiveness. Because there are no more blood sacrifices being made for sins, we must conclude then that the one-time blood sacrifice of Jesus Christ was sufficient to bring a lifetime of forgiveness. Four times in the New Testament is the phrase "once for all," speaking of the sacrifice of Jesus on the cross. It is not an over and over forgiveness that we have, but a once for all forgiveness. In John 19:30, Jesus said, "It is finished." He did not say that it is half finished. Jesus Christ was the Lamb of God that "took away the sin of the world."

> [23] *It was necessary, then, for the copies of the heavenly things to be purified with these sacrifices, but the heavenly things themselves with better sacrifices than these.* [24] *For Christ did not enter a man-*

made sanctuary that was only a copy of the true one; he entered heaven itself, now to appear for us in God's presence. ²⁵ Nor did he enter heaven to offer himself again and again, the way the high priest enters the Most Holy Place every year with blood that is not his own. ²⁶ Then Christ would have had to suffer many times since the creation of the world. But now he has appeared once for all at the end of the ages to do away with sin by the sacrifice of himself. (Hebrews 9:23-26 NIV)

If Christ did not enter heaven to offer Himself again and again, then we're not down here getting forgiven over and over again. What is true there is true here. If it's finished in heaven, then it's finished on earth. It's not again and again forgiveness, but once for all forgiveness.

The Old Covenant was an unfinished work. The New Covenant is a finished work.

¹¹ And every priest stands ministering daily and offering repeatedly the same sacrifices, which can never take away sins. ¹² But this Man, after He had offered one sacrifice for sins forever, sat down at the right hand of God, (Hebrews 10:11-12)

The reason the Old Testament priest stands daily is that it is an unfinished work that could never take away sin. But Jesus, after He offered one sacrifice for sin FOREVER, sat down. Why did He sit down? Because His Work was finished. Sin had been removed!

Are you seated with Christ (Ephesians 2:6), or are you standing? Are you resting in the finished work of Christ, or are you running around trying to do or say something to get God to forgive you? There are only two realities regarding your sin. Either you are seated in Him or you are standing up.

Under the Old Covenant system, there was a constant reminder of sins every year, but today in many of our churches, Christians are reminded of their sins every Sunday. The way to overcome our sin is not to focus on our sin, but to focus on Jesus Christ. We have been invited to depend on that one-time sacrifice as the means of eternal redemption, lifelong forgiveness of sin. Any method we have that begins with us doing something to defeat sin is hopeless. Jesus already defeated sin. I'm not minimizing sin. I'm magnifying Jesus. People who want you to focus on your sin minimize sin. They are saying that sin is so weak that you can defeat it by religious self-discipline.

Christ Conscious, Not Sin Conscious

I hear this statement often, "The problem with the church today is that we are not sin conscious enough. We need more preaching on sin." Most every church I know is preaching against sin every Sunday. Every weekend, you are reminded of your sins. This mixed message comes with the pressure to perform and the fear that comes from failure. You make promises to God, and then you break them. You promise to try harder, only to fail again. Sunday, for many, just becomes a weekly meeting where our sinfulness is proclaimed. We feel guilt and condemnation, confess our sins, and go out to live another week as a defeated sin conscious Christian. You get worn out. Don't ever buy into any message that causes you to trust in yourself and your works instead of Jesus and His Works.

When you hear the New Covenant of Grace preached, it is always Christ exalting. It always reveals more and more of Jesus. There is no grace without Jesus. It makes you Christ conscious, not sin conscious. It is not making little of sin, but much of Jesus.

Where the Law is preached, they call your sin to remembrance, but where the New Covenant is preached, your righteousness is called to remembrance. The emphasis is not on what you must do but on what Jesus has done. Not on your obedience, but on His Obedience. Not on your righteousness, but on His Righteousness. The message of grace will turn your eyes away from yourself to look upon Jesus, the author and finisher of your faith.

I have a question: How much time do you spend thinking about a bill that you have already paid in full? I would say, none. I would say that you are no longer "bill conscious." Why? Because the debt is gone. It has been removed. If your sin was paid for by the sacrifice of Jesus Christ on the cross, then you have no sin debt. You should have no more consciousness of sin. We are in a New Covenant. A key promise of this New Covenant is *"their sins and lawless deed I will remember no more"* (Hebrews 10:16-17). The reason the Old Covenant did not work is that it was dependent upon the obedience of the people to the Law of God. The New Covenant is dependent upon Christ and His Obedience, His Righteousness. If you are in Christ, you are in this New Covenant that has taken sin out of the way. God does not remember your sin anymore.

As I said in the introduction of this book, the issue is not your sin. You will sin, but the issue is what you believe when you sin. What do you do when you blow it? Do you hide from God, or do you run to Him? When you sin, don't focus on your sin, but fix your eyes on Jesus.

I'm not saying the sinning does not matter. The New Testament warns us about the dangers of sin. WHY? Not to make you doubt God's forgiveness or grace, but to warn us of the consequences of sin. Sin grieves our Father who loves us. When we hurt ourselves, or hurt others by sin, it hurts Him. But God is not holding our sins against us. Sin can hurt you, make you sick, and grieve the Holy Spirit, but one thing sin cannot do is undo the finished work of Jesus Christ on the cross and cause God to UN-FORGIVE you. No matter how great your sin is HIS grace is still greater! There is nothing you can do to make God love you more or nothing you can do to make Him love you less. God didn't start loving you when you received Christ. While we were sinners, God demonstrated His Love for us. My actions will not change God's heart toward me, but my sins will affect my heart toward God. It will not cause Him to love me less, but my sin will cause me to love Him less.

When you understand God's grace, His Forgiveness, His unearned favor, you will no longer have a consciousness of sin, for you will be Christ conscious. You will look to Him as your only source for overcoming victory.

Chapter 6

Myth: Christians Need to Constantly Confess Their Sins to God to Remain Forgiven

If you have been raised in church, you will likely have a problem as I present forgiveness the way the Bible teaches it. Christians needing to constantly confess their sins is such a common myth and is so ingrained in the church today that it may offend or anger you for me to even suggest otherwise. By believing this myth, many believers' lives have been reduced to nothing more than a sin management program.

It is vital to understand complete forgiveness. One thing I see now is that I lived so many years as a believer, not believing or understanding that I had been completely forgiven of all sin. Because of this, I had no real confidence in my relationship with God. When I sinned, I would confess that sin and plead with Him to forgive me. Depending upon what I deemed the severity of the sin, I would ask God over and over to please forgive me of my sin. Sometimes for multiple days, I would ask Him to forgive me.

The church had taught me that I needed to keep a "short sin account" with God, not realizing that God was not keeping a ledger book of my sins. Forgiveness simply means that God is not counting your sins against you. Forgiveness is the cancellation of a debt. If you believe that God keeps a record of your sin and holds a sin-debt against you, then it makes sense to ask Him to forgive you your debt. However, I choose to believe the Bible.

> *God was reconciling the world to himself in Christ, not counting men's sins against them. And He has committed to us the message of reconciliation.* (2 Corinthians 5:19 NIV)

> *¹⁷ then He adds, "Their sins and their lawless deeds I will remember no more." (Hebrews 10:17-18 NIV)*

> *²⁹ The next day John saw Jesus coming toward him, and said, "Behold! The Lamb of God who takes away the sin of the world!* (John 1:29 NIV)

> *² And He Himself is the propitiation for our sins, and not for ours only but also for the whole world. (1 John 2:2 NIV)*

Jesus didn't just take away the sins of the churchgoers. He took away the sins of the whole world. The sinner is forgiven and accepted before he ever asks God for forgiveness. That's good news, yet most Christians have never heard it. This muddled message keeps Christians busy pursuing God for what they already possess – HIS forgiveness. Many of us are inconsistent in our beliefs. We say, "Jesus took my sins away, but He still needs to take my sins away. Yes, Jesus forgave me, but He still needs to forgive me. Jesus said it is finished, but it is still not finished." You won't find any person in the New Testament confessing their sins in order to be forgiven. Why didn't Jesus say to the woman caught in adultery in John 8, "Confess your sin"? Why did He say to the paralytic man in Luke 5:20, *"Be of good cheer; your sins are forgiven you"*? The man hadn't confessed his sins, how then could he be forgiven? Notice the man had not repented. He had not confessed his sins. He had not even asked for forgiveness.

The scribes and Pharisees got upset about this, and they still get upset about this today. Why did Jesus tell him that his sins ARE forgiven, not will be forgiven if he repents or confesses? This man had come to be healed, yet Jesus pronounced him forgiven. If Jesus said something or did something, there was a reason, a need for it. He never just spoke things to be speaking. There was divine purpose behind everything He said. This man needed to hear "Your sins are forgiven you." The world today needs to hear this same message. You need to hear this – your sins are forgiven you! Receive this revelation that all your sins have been forgiven. This belief affects your healing, your health, every area of your life!

I've been asked, "Why don't we see more healings today?" Because of the lack of proclamation that your sins are forgiven you. People don't have faith and confidence to receive freely what grace has provided. They think that their sin is hindering God from healing them.

Am I saying it is wrong to confess your sins as a believer? NO. You can talk to your heavenly Father about anything, including your sin. But it is wrong to believe that you must confess your sins in order to be forgiven. It is wrong to tell people that God will not forgive them unless they repent or confess their sins one by one. It's wrong to put a price tag on what is free – God's grace. Jesus *took away the sin of the whole world* (John 1:29). Did Jesus succeed? Do you believe it?

Listen to Paul preach. After the resurrection, forgiveness of sins is a done deal.

> [38] *Therefore let it be known to you, brethren, that through this Man is preached to you the forgiveness of sins;* [39] *and by Him everyone who believes is justified from all things from which you could not be justified by the law of Moses.* (Acts 13:38-39)

> [7] *In Him we have redemption through His blood, the forgiveness of sins, according to the riches of His grace* (Ephesians 1:7)

> [13] *He has delivered us from the power of darkness and conveyed us into the kingdom of the Son of His love,* [14] *in whom we have redemption through His blood, the forgiveness of sins.* (Colossians 1:13-14)

> [12] *I write to you, little children, Because your sins are forgiven you for His name's sake.* (1 John 2:12)

Notice John says your sins ARE forgiven you, not will be forgiven when you confess them. If I believe that I must confess my sins to be forgiven, then I have to disbelieve that Jesus took away the sin on the world. If I believe that God has not forgiven me, then I accuse God of the sin of harboring unforgiveness, which is in itself a sin. The Bible teaches that we are not supposed to wait until those who sin against us repent and confess before we forgive them. Right?

> *[13] bearing with one another, and forgiving one another, if anyone has a complaint against another; even as Christ forgave you, so you also must do.* (Colossians 3:13)

Did not Jesus on the cross forgive those who had not asked for forgiveness, repented, or confessed their sins? **God does not need your permission to forgive you your sin against Him!** I have forgiven many people of their sins against me, and they have never asked for it. Some do not even desire it, but I forgave them anyway. I did not need their permission.

Am I saying that since all have been forgiven of sin that everyone is saved? NO! You are forgiven, but you will not experience it until you receive His Forgiveness by receiving Jesus as your savior. The scriptures say, *"But as many as **received Him**, to them He gave the right to become children of God"* (John 1:12).

When you preach God's unconditional love and forgiveness of sin, it's easy for some to say, "Well, that's universalism." A Universalist is a person who believes all will be saved. I do believe in universal love, and I believe in universal forgiveness. But I do not believe everyone is saved. I do believe everyone's sins have been forgiven. Just a thought, how can you have universal love (that all the church believes) and conditional forgiveness? How can you believe that God loves everybody and yet He has only forgiven a select few? How can you truly love a person that you have not forgiven?

Herein lies a problem. Many in the church do not really understand salvation. Ask the average Christian how to be saved, and most will tell you to "confess your sins to God, ask God to forgive you, say the 'sinners' prayer." Most will tell you that being a Christian means that their sins have been forgiven; however, forgiveness does not equal salvation. God has forgiven the sin of the world, but the whole world is not saved. Salvation is not only that we're forgiven, but that we now have "life". The issue was not that Adam sinned in the garden and needed forgiveness. It was that Adam died and needed life.

Jesus said He came that we might have Life! Salvation is the cross and the empty tomb. It is crucifixion and resurrection. Salvation happens when we receive not only the benefit of His Forgiveness, but also His Life.

When the jailer in Acts 16:30 asked Paul, "What must I do to be saved?" notice Paul does not even mention the word "sin". He simply tells him to believe in the Lord Jesus and you will be saved. This is very different from what most of today's churches are saying. In Romans 10:9-10, there are classic verses with instruction on how to be saved, and there is no mention of the word "sin". Why? Because your sins are not the issue. They have already been forgiven. JESUS is the issue. The issue is Life!

Whenever I teach that all your sins have been forgiven, invariably someone will bring up 1John 1:9 as their proof text that we must confess our sins in order to be forgiven. The reason this verse is quoted is that it is the only verse in the whole New Testament that seems to link the confession of sin with God's forgiveness. It is amazing how people who say you must confess your sins in order to be forgiven will grab hold of 1John 1:9 while they ignore all the other verses in the New Testament that clearly teach that all our sins have been forgiven. There is a clear explanation for this often-misunderstood passage. Context is everything in the Bible. Take a verse out of context and your left with just "con." Let's look at this verse in context:

> *⁸ If we say that we have no sin, we deceive ourselves, and the truth is not in us. ⁹ If we confess our sins, He is faithful and just to forgive us our sins and to cleanse us from all unrighteousness. ¹⁰ If we say that we have not sinned, we make Him a liar, and His word is not in us.* (1 John 1:8-10)

In chapter one of 1 John, he is clearly speaking to unbelievers. John tells us in verse 3 that he writes it to those (lost) who do not yet have fellowship with the Father or His Son Jesus Christ. Verse 9 is aimed at "sin deniers," people who were deceived, who say they have NO sin. They deny that sin even exists. This is not a verse that teaches the work of Christ is not finished. In verse eight, they say they have NO sin, that they were deceived. John was telling them that if they would confess that they had sin, they could experience God's forgiveness and cleansing. In verse nine, he says that God would cleanse them from all unrighteousness. This is another proof that he is talking to sinners. The Bible never refers to the saved as unrighteous. In verse 10, they were calling God a liar by denying that sin was real. This is the very reason Jesus came – to shed His Blood and to take away the sin of the world. They were saying that Jesus did not need to come because sin did not exist.

Then in chapter 2 of 1 John, he begins with the phrase, "My little children." He is addressing believers, and in 1 John 2:12, he writes:

> *¹² I write to you, little children, because **your sins are forgiven you** for His name's sake.*

Notice he tells them their sins are forgiven. He doesn't say "if you will confess them." Did Jesus cleanse us from *all* sin or only *some* sin (specifically the sin we confess)? Does He cleanse us from *all* unrighteousness or only *some* unrighteousness? Here John is unequivocal. Jesus cleanses us from "*all* unrighteousness" (verse 9).

If you believe being forgiven by God is dependent upon your confession, then you believe a myth that will keep you in bondage. But if you believe what the New Testament teaches, that all your sins have been forgiven, you will live Christ conscious and not sin conscious. As you focus on Jesus and His Grace, you can't help but walk in faith and victory.

Chapter 7

Myth: Only Our Past Sins Are Forgiven

I was taught that only my past sins—from the day I was born until the day I became a Christian—have been forgiven, and that my future sins are not forgiven until I confess them and seek forgiveness. I was taught that I had to be careful how I lived because if the rapture occurred right after I had sinned, I would be left behind, or if I died suddenly before repenting, then I would be lost. When were you and I actually forgiven of our sins? Two thousand years ago, when Jesus shed His Blood. You "received" forgiveness when you believed, but your forgiveness happened when Jesus' blood was shed. How many of our sins were future sins when Jesus died on the cross? ALL OF THEM! If Jesus' blood didn't take away all sin, including future sins, then we are all still lost because all our sins were future sins when He died. So, if you are not forgiven of **all sin**, then you are not forgiven at all.

One of the Bible's greatest truths is that Christ died to take away all sins, not just part of them, but all of them: past, present, and future. He took away not just the sins of the Christians, but the sins of the whole world (1 John 2:2). In Colossians 2:13, Paul wrote, *"He forgave us all our sins."* The Greek word translated to "all" in English means "each and every, any and all." When we are born again, **all** our past, present, and future sins are forgiven. The Bible says that Christ *"appeared once for all at the end of the ages to do away with sin by the sacrifice of himself"* (Hebrews 9:26). The question is did Jesus do away with all sin or just some sin? Jesus forgave all your sins at the cross long before you were born, long before you did anything. It's a simple truth, yet many believers don't know it.

> *[8] For if these things are yours and abound, you will be neither barren nor unfruitful in the knowledge of our Lord Jesus Christ. [9] For he who lacks these things is shortsighted, even to blindness, and has forgotten that he was cleansed from his old sins.* (2 Peter 1:8-9)

Peter writes that the main reason Christians are unfruitful in their lives is that they have forgotten that they have been cleansed from their sin problem. Their knowledge of what Jesus accomplished is so limited that they are "shortsighted and blind." They live powerless lives. Some actually try to use this verse as a proof text that only old or past sins are forgiven. How foolish! The word "sins" here, as in most places in the New Testament, is a noun and not a verb. It is a thing and not an action. I love the Message translation of this verse.

Without these qualities you can't see what's right before you, oblivious that your old sinful life has been wiped off the books. (2 Peter 1:9 MSG)

The use of "old" here is about the old man, your old life.

To keep a Christian fearful, weak, and powerless, the enemy only needs to get us to believe that Jesus only forgave our past sins and that it's up to us to maintain our forgiveness. This myth says that God has only half-forgiven us. Don't believe this lie. Jesus forgave us at the cross. If you sin, you can always tell God about it without feeling condemned because you know that you already have total and complete forgiveness because of the blood of Jesus! ALL our sins have been forgiven. Past, present, and future!

Chapter 8

Myth: Grace Is Simply a Licence to Sin

It seems that in some Christian circles the word "grace" has become a swear word. I remember hearing preachers use the phrase "greasy grace" as they spoke about grace as a license to sin. But despite all this opposition to grace, let's be clear. Whether you like it or not, the Bible teaches that God's solution for sin is His Grace released through the cross. Grace is the one thing that sets Christianity apart from all other religions in the world. It is not turning from sin, prayer, confession, moral living. It is grace. To say that grace is just a license to sin is to say that God sent the wrong remedy for the problem of sin.

For the law was given through Moses, but grace and truth came through Jesus Christ. (John 1: 17)

Trying to separate Jesus from grace is like trying to separate wet from water. Grace is not a doctrine. Grace is a Person, and His name is Jesus! Saying that grace is a license to sin is saying that Jesus is a license to sin. To say grace promotes sin is saying Jesus promotes sin. Jesus is God's Grace! Grace isn't permission to sin, but the power to sin no more. In Romans 6:14, Paul said, *"For sin shall not have dominion over you: for you are not under the law, but under grace."* Grace breaks sin's dominion over us. The Law, or a performance-based message, gives sin dominion over us. The statement that Grace is a license to sin is a lie that causes people to be leery of the only message that can empower them to go and sin no more. The Grace of God actually teaches us to say NO to sin, not yes to sin.

> [11] *For the Grace of God that brings salvation has appeared to all men.* [12] *It teaches us to say "No" to ungodliness and worldly passions, and to live self-controlled, upright and godly lives in this present age.* (Titus 2:11-12 NIV)

His Grace teaches us to say no to sin. Notice, it's not the Law that teaches us to say no to sin. It's not the Ten Commandments that teach us to say no to sin. It is God's Grace! If the grace you're feeding from teaches you to say yes to sin, then it's not the Grace of God. The revelation of grace will never produce a sinful lifestyle. On the contrary, it will set you free from a lifestyle of sin. Grace teaches us to live holy lives. Holiness is a fruit and not a root of salvation (Romans 6:22). Our holiness is a response to God's grace, not something we do to earn God's grace. Grace cannot be earned, or it wouldn't be grace (Romans 11:6). When we clearly see the grace that God has extended to us, the love of God will abound in our lives, and we will accidentally live more holy lives than we ever have before on purpose.

There is no better test that a preacher is really preaching the Gospel of Grace than the fact that some will misunderstand and misinterpret the message as an endorsement to sin. If we preach God's grace as Paul did, we will have to defend the message as Paul did.

> *¹What shall we say then? Shall we continue in sin that grace may abound? ²Certainly not! How shall we who died to sin live any longer in it?* (Romans 6:1-2)

Paul addressed that very question four times in the book of Romans. This question normally never comes up in most churches today. Why? Because the true Gospel that Paul preached is not being presented.

Well, can't the grace message be abused? Yes, but many other messages can be abused as well. The answer to error is not to abandon the truth, but to hold to the truth. We're to respond to truth, but we're not to react to fear as this often creates more error. People who have listened to preaching that mixes Law and grace often see God as their judge and not their Father.

The issue for the abuser of grace is not their behavior but their identity. There is a huge difference between pursing grace for what you can get out of it and chasing grace for Who grace is. As with any truth from God, a minority of people will misunderstand and abuse God's Amazing Grace. We should never allow the abuse of some to cause us to back away from God's grace. Don't ever fall for the lie that says, "I can go on sinning so that grace may abound."

It is true that your sinning won't affect God's love for you, but it will affect your love for Him. Your sinning won't cause God to love you less, but it causes you to love Him less. It will enslave you and harden your heart. This is not God's will for your life.

> *What shall we say then? Shall we continue in sin, that grace may abound? God forbid.* (Romans 6:1)

I realize that some use this scripture to condemn those who are struggling to overcome sin. If you are troubled when you sin ... good. Your discomfort is actually a sign of the new nature and God's desires within you. However, if you sin and are not troubled ... bad. Maybe you think grace is a license to sin. Something is very wrong here. I've always been amazed that people would complain that the grace message is a license to sin. I've found the word "license" interesting. Since when do we need a license to sin? The statement I've heard again and again goes something like this: "If God's grace is the way you say it is, then what stops me from sinning like crazy? You mean that I can sin, and if I die, I'll still go to heaven?"

Why would you immediately jump to that conclusion after hearing that we are forgiven for everything and He will never leave us or forsake us? Could you imagine going to a wedding and listening to the bride and groom recite their vows: "I commit to you forever. Through sickness and health. For richer or poorer. For better or for worse. Till death do us part." After the wedding, some guy tells the groom that her vows meant "you can live any way you want to now, you can cheat on her, get drunk, or whatever." You say, that's foolishness! Exactly! But that is basically what we're saying about our forever covenant with God when we think that it's a license to sin.

The difference between those who get it and those who don't is love. People who do not have love in their hearts almost always interpret a forever covenant as an opportunity to sin. It's no surprise to me that when the grace message is preached, the first thing that comes to mind in the average Christian is sin. Most churches are preaching behavior modification and talk about sinning less. Finding out that God loves you whether you sin or not is too scary for most Christians because they aren't sure what they'd do with that kind of freedom.

> *¹ It is for freedom that Christ has set us free.* (Galatians 5:1 NIV)

When you give a person their freedom, you are giving them the opportunity to choose. The church today is terrified for people to have this power to choose. I've heard people say, "You can't preach grace to new believers. They are not mature enough to handle that kind of freedom. Removing the Law from believers will cause them to sin more. I know freedom frightens Law preachers because at the end of the day they believe more in the power of sin than the power of the Cross. Sin is powerful, but Christ is much more powerful. I'm not making little of sin, but I am making much of Jesus! Where the Spirit of the Lord is, there is freedom. In Christ, we preach HIS gospel of grace and kingdom (Acts 20:24), and we hand out licenses of freedom from sin, not freedom to sin. We are forgiven and have freedom from both the slavery to sin and death. We are now citizens of a new Kingdom, with a new King – and by His Spirit we live. Let these truths about the Gospel of God's grace dispel the myth that grace is a license to sin. I promise you that these truths will transform your life. Have faith in God – His Grace is powerful!

Chapter 9

Myth: We Need to Bombard Heaven with Our Prayers

In my many years now as a believer, I have discovered that there is a huge difference between the traditional view of prayer and what the Bible teaches. Most of us have been taught that if we just pray long and hard enough and not give up, God will eventually answer our prayers. Phrases like "We need to bombard heaven," or "We need to storm the gates of heaven and give God no rest," all reflect our view that we need to wear God down. Others think that God is moved to answer by the number of people praying for their need, so they try to get as many people as possible praying for their need. Maybe then, God will answer. They believe there is strength in numbers. This is the logic behind prayer chains and all-night prayer events. If we can get enough people praying around the clock, God will then be touched by our perseverance and answer our prayers.

Don't misunderstand me. I'm not saying that there's anything wrong with asking people to pray with you concerning your need. The Bible encourages us to pray for one another. What I am saying is that praying is NOT begging. Prayer is NOT us trying to convince God that we need help. The way we pray reflects how we view God. The reason many peoples' prayers are ineffective is their view of God is wrong. They see God as this adversarial god who must be badgered and begged, or they think that He is too busy running the universe to be bothered by you and your needs. That's not true. Our God is not some uncaring judge who must be begged to move on our behalf. That's ridiculous and blasphemous. Our Father loves us and will respond to our prayers. What if you came to my house and observed my children begging me to give them something to eat and I just ignored them. They cried out to me and said, "Please, Daddy, I know I didn't clean my room this morning, but please have mercy on me and give me some food." If you saw this, you would call social services on me! Of course, I wouldn't treat my children like this and neither would any father. Why do you think God would treat you that way?

> *So I say to you, ask, and it will be given to you; seek, and you will find; knock, and it will be opened to you. For everyone who asks receives, and he who seeks finds, and to him who knocks it will be opened. If a son asks for bread from any father among you, will he give him a stone? Or if he asks for a fish, will he give him a serpent instead of a fish? Or if he asks for an egg, will he offer him a scorpion? If you then, being evil, know how to give good gifts to your children, how*

much more will your heavenly Father give the Holy Spirit to those who ask Him! (Luke 11:9-13)

In the above verses, Jesus is saying that if evil earthly fathers will provide for their children and not hurt them, our Good and Gracious Heavenly Father will provide much more for us and not hurt us! A loving Father could do no less! If your son asks for bread because he is hungry, would you give him a stone to eat? A stone that would break his teeth and hurt him. If he asked for fish, would you give him a snake to bite him and hurt him? If he asked for an egg, would you give him a scorpion to sting him and hurt him? Of course not! God will not hurt you either. You won't ask for one thing and receive something else. Where did we ever come up with these wrong views of God and prayer in the first place? I'm sad to say in church. Most of us have been given a wrong view of God and prayer from two of Jesus' parables. In Luke 11:5-8 and in Luke 18:1-8, Jesus gave two parables that illustrate the heart of the Father toward us.

Most preachers have used these two parables to teach us that you must beg and plead with God to get Him to answer your prayers, when actually Jesus is teaching the opposite. Jesus was making an argument through contrast. He was not giving a comparison. In Luke 11, He talks about a person who is supposed to be a friend to a man who comes to him at midnight with a need. The man refuses to get out of bed and help his friend, but because the man will not leave him alone, eventually the "friend" reluctantly gets up and grants his request. Jesus was not teaching that this is the way the Father is. He was saying that God would not treat you like this. He said just ask and you will receive!

In Luke 18, Jesus tells a parable about a judge who "did not fear God nor regard man." This judge wasn't loving or caring. He was indifferent to the plight of the widow woman, yet he was eventually worn down by her persistent begging. This is the way the average Christian sees God as one you must badger and beg. And if you will give Him no rest, you can eventually wear Him down into submission to your desire. What a joke!

The truth is that Jesus was not making a comparison but a contrast. He was saying that if a wicked, uncaring judge will answer her prayer, how much will God answer our prayers!

> *Then the Lord said, "Hear what the **unjust judge** said. And* ***shall God not avenge His own*** *elect who cry out day and night to Him, though He bears long with them? I tell you that **He will avenge them speedily**. Nevertheless, when the Son of Man comes, will He really find faith on the earth?"* (Luke 18:6-8)

Do you see it? God not only said that He would avenge His own, but also that He would do it quickly! Praise God! God is not reluctant to answer you like the unjust judge. That's the problem. The average Christian sees God as their judge. If you've been born again, He's your Father, not your judge. Our relationship to God is not judicial. God is not sitting on a throne of judgment toward you, but on a throne of grace, where you are to come boldly and find help in time of need (Hebrews 4:16). You can approach God boldly knowing that He doesn't have to be persuaded to care about you and your request.

Many people think that prayer is to inform God of our crisis. He already knows your need before you ask Him (Matthew 6:8). Some of us think that if we tell God how pitiful our situation is,

He will answer our prayer because of our desperate circumstances. Desperation is not the same thing as faith. Faith works by love! God is not moved by how desperate your situation is, but because of His Love for you and your faith in Him. God is not moved by the number of people that you have praying. You don't have to come with a prayer petition signed by hundreds of people to convince God to rule in your favor. Your heavenly Father is already on your side. He is for you, not against you. You need to know that. **There is nothing you can do or pray to make god more disposed to you than what Jesus has already done. God loves you!** Prayer is simply receiving by your faith in His Goodness what His Grace has already provided. That's the truth of His Amazing Grace!

Chapter 10

Myth: Believers Still Have a Sinful Nature

Many believers think that it's their nature to sin, and therefore, they need to die to themselves. But that's simply not true! You died already. You are not a saint with a sinful nature any more than you could be a sinner with a saintful nature. Every believer knows that Jesus died on the cross **for** them, but few believers know that Jesus died **as** them.

"We died with Christ…" (Romans 6:8)

"You died with Christ…" (Colossians 2:20a)

"For you died…" (Colossians 3:3a)

> *We judge thus: That if One died for all, then all died.*
> (2 Corinthians 5:14)

In Romans 6, Paul says that our old sinful nature was completely removed. At salvation, a Christian's sinful nature is crucified and buried with Christ:

> *...knowing this, that our old man* [sinful nature] *was crucified with Him, that the body of sin might be done away with, that we should no longer be slaves of sin. (*Romans 6:6, annotations added)

After we are born again, we are not "sinners" anymore, even though we sometimes sin. There is not one verse in the entire New Covenant that calls a born-again believer a "sinner". The term "sinner" refers to a person who has not yet been born again. (This is consistent throughout the New Testament after the cross.) And yet, we find most Christians today thinking, "I am still a sinner with a sin nature."

The problem with this myth is it implies that a Christian still has two natures. The Bible teaches that at the cross our old nature was crucified with Christ. It's not there, because it was put to death. It's no longer our nature to sin. You may have a sin habit, but you do not have a sin nature. You may at times of weakness yield to temptation, but that has nothing to do with you having a sin nature.

If after salvation you still have two natures, then you would be set up for constant failure. Jesus said that a house divided against itself cannot stand. You're not some kind of spiritual split personality like Jekyll & Hyde. Your heart is not a "duplex" where two very different natures try to coexist. Your loving Father would not place you in such a hopeless condition.

The expression "sinful nature" or "sin nature" does not even occur in the Bible, NKJV, or KJV.

You do, however, find that phrase used over fifty times in the NIV translation. Now the NIV is one of the English Bibles that I use at times, but its translators made a regrettable misinterpretation of the Greek word "sarx" (which translated means "flesh"). Most of us have heard the doctrine of the "sin nature" preached to us in church with amazing conviction. It has caused sincere believers to think that they have a sin nature that seeks to rise up and take control. This makes them feel helpless and frustrated, with no power to live a righteous lifestyle. It fills them with a lack of confidence before God and an expectation of punishment by God.

Once you have put your faith in Christ and are born again, your sin nature is dead. You have died to your sinful nature and are now alive "in Christ." You are now a new creation.

> *"If anyone is in Christ, he is a new creation; old things have passed away; behold, all things have become new."* (2 Corinthians 5:17)

Your old self, your old nature has "passed away." It is not that we just **received** something new. No, we **became** something new! The new nature is not added to the old nature. It replaces it. All things "have become new." It's a finished work! You no longer have a sinful nature. Now you have been made a partaker of the divine nature.

> *"by which have been given to us exceedingly great and precious promises, that through these you may be partakers of the **divine nature**, having escaped the corruption that is in the world through lust."* (2 Peter 1:4)

If we can truly understand and believe that Christ lives in us and that we have a new nature in Him, then it will empower us to walk in freedom. You truly have become a partaker of His Divine Nature. The proof of this is your new desires. You still have the capacity to sin, but you no longer have the capacity to enjoy sin. Sinning makes you miserable. It's not who you are any longer.

So Why Do I Still Sin?

If God completely removed our sinful nature, why then do we still sin? The answers are numerous. We sin because of our unrenewed minds and because we yield to the external temptations of our flesh. Many continue to struggle with sin because they believe the myth that they are sinners still at their core. Belief determines behavior. Christians will not act in a way that contradicts what they truly believe about themselves. Some sin out of habit, and others may do it out of ignorance. The fact is that Christians still sin. But the truth is our nature has been changed. The only reason that many still sin is because they don't know these truths (John 8:32).

When we are born again, we become totally new in our spirits. This old nature has been completely changed (2 Corinthians 5:17). It's not in the process of becoming new. It's already as pure and perfect as Jesus (1 John 4:17, 1 Corinthians 6:17, and Ephesians 4:24). Our sin nature is gone, but we still live in a body. That body is of the carnal mind. It will still function as programmed until we reprogram it. That's what the Bible calls the renewing of the mind. True transformation only comes by the renewing of our minds (Romans 12:2). Victory in the Christian life is as simple as renewing our minds to who we are and what we have already received in Christ. It's not the struggle of two natures inside of us. We are the way we think we are (Proverbs 23:7). If we see ourselves as having a sin nature, then we will continue to struggle with sin. But, if we see the total change that took place in our nature, we will manifest that change in our lives and actions.

Chapter 11

Myth: Grace and Truth Must Be Kept in Balance

For the law was given through Moses, but grace and truth came through Jesus Christ. (John 1:17)

The very idea that you could and should balance grace and truth speaks of grace and truth as though they are two distinct and separate things. It is not grace OR truth. It is both grace AND truth. Does the Bible teach us this separation? Absolutely not! Trying to separate grace from truth is like trying to separate wet from water. You can't do it. It's impossible. When we try to separate grace from truth, we get a perverted version of grace.

Grace is truth, and truth is grace. Truth is a Person, and grace is a Person. Jesus is truth, and Jesus is grace. Jesus is not part grace and part truth. He is all grace and all truth. He does not need to be "balanced". He is perfect. Jesus did not come to merely show us grace, but to be grace. When we try to separate truth from grace, we get the Old Covenant of the Law. We end up trying to fulfill the Law in our own strength and ability, and the enemy uses this to produce pride in us when we've done right, condemnation when we've done wrong, and eventually hopelessness and a hardened angry heart towards God, the gospel, and the church.

Usually when someone is concerned about balancing grace and truth, it is because they see the "truth" as the Law. They fear the undiluted Grace of God. You will hear statements like "You need to be careful about grace. Grace needs to be balanced with the Law. Be careful of these 'hyper-grace' preachers." Why don't you ever hear "You better be careful about those Law preachers"? I grew up in church hearing the phrase "greasy grace," as if grace was something bad. When grace is questioned, we're insulting God.

*And the Word became flesh and dwelt among us, and we beheld His glory, the glory as of the only begotten of the Father, **full of grace and truth**.* (John 1:14)

Jesus came full of grace and truth. Did God send the wrong solution to the dilemma of sin? Do we actually believe in a New Covenant that not only allows sin, but promotes sin? Preachers are afraid of grace because they think it discourages obedience and encourages sin. I've noticed that attacks on grace always come from those inside the church. They fear that grace does not possess the teeth to keep folks "in-line." As a result, most of us who grew up in church did so on a steady diet of "do more, try harder" sermons. Those preachers think this will cause people to clean up their act, to sin less, to volunteer in the nursery, to read their Bibles. But it actually has the opposite effect. A steady diet of "do more, try harder" sermons doesn't cause people to do more or try harder … it makes them give up.

What Grace Is Not and What Grace Is

Grace is **not** a very important doctrine. Grace is **not** another subject of the Bible. GRACE IS the subject of the Bible. I hear ministers say, "Over the next eight weeks, we're going to focus on grace." I think, "What have they been focusing on?" Grace is a Person. Grace is everything Jesus. Grace saved you, and His name is Jesus. Not a doctrine or teaching about Jesus, but by Jesus Himself. Our Father sits on a throne of grace. We are made righteous by grace, kept by grace, and empowered to "go and sin no more" by His Amazing Grace. Grace is truth, and truth is grace. They are in perfect harmony. Don't believe the myth. There's nothing to balance, no contrast between grace and truth. Jesus Christ is "full of grace and truth!"

Chapter 12

Myth: You Need to Love God More

I grew up in church hearing that our greatest need is to love God more. "Our problem is we don't love God enough." I heard this preached often as the reason for "worldliness" in the church. They would quote or should I say misquote 1 John 2:15.

> *Do not love the world or the things in the world. If anyone loves the world, the **love of the Father** is not in him.* (1 John 2:15)

Notice the verse says the love OF the Father, not the love FOR the Father. This is the reason we yield to temptation. We lack the revelation of the Father's love for us. Let me ask you a question. Do you feel that you love God enough? Do you feel that you ought to love Him more than you do? If so, why don't you? The answer is simple, you can't! It isn't possible to love Him more until we first know how much He loves us.

We love Him because He first loved us. (1 John 4:19)

This verse tells me that we were incapable of loving Him before we received His Love for us. The direction of love is not from earth toward heaven, rather from heaven toward earth. God so loved the world, that He gave His Son (John 3:16). We are not trying to get God to love us. He loved us while we were yet sinners (Romans 5:8). The point is that our focus should be on God's love for us and not our love for Him.

Some may be thinking, "Doesn't the New Testament command us to love God?"

"Teacher, which is the great commandment in the law?" Jesus said to him, "'You shall love the LORD your God with all your heart, with all your soul, and with all your mind." This is the first and great commandment. (Matthew 22:36-38)

Jesus didn't give the commandment here for us to keep today. He was asked a question about the Law, and He answered it. Have you ever prayed for God to help you love Him more? Then that is proof that you felt you were falling short. I made this commandment my daily prayer for years. I would ask God to help me fulfill this command – to love God with all my heart, all my soul, and all my mind. I just knew that all my problems could be answered if I just loved God more.

Have you ever prayed like that? What's wrong with us wanting to love God more? There's nothing wrong with wanting to love God more, but our approach is the problem. I had somehow always missed the word "law". I was asking God to help me fulfill or keep the Law. No man can keep the Law. There was only one who kept the Law and fulfilled it, and that one man was Jesus.

Commanding people to love does not work. Just try to command people to love one another and see how that works out for you. It might be good, but it's not possible.

Our love for God is not something that we can simply initiate. Our love for Him grows as a response to our revelation of His Love for us. This is the "because" of why we love Him. When we stop trying to love God by our efforts and simply focus on how much He loves us, then we grow in our love for Him.

Some say that the definition of love is found in 1 Corinthians 13:4. "Love is patient, love is kind." No, those are the characteristics of love. There is a definition of love found in 1 John 4:10.

> **In this is love, not that we loved God, but that He loved us** *and sent His Son to be the propitiation for our sins.* (1 John 4:10)

Notice John said, "This is love, not that we loved God." John received a revelation that we desperately need. John had come into the revelation of God's Grace, not that we loved Him (the Law), but that He loved us (grace). In John 19:26, John refers to himself as "the disciple whom He loved." John finally got the revelation of God's love for Him. Where did he get it? Looking at the cross. John, in the closing chapters of the book of John, referred to himself five times as the disciple whom Jesus loved. He knew it was not about his love for Jesus, but Jesus' love for him. It was a complete shift in his identity and how he saw himself.

Jesus lived in the revelation that He was loved by His Father. His Father spoke audibly at His baptism and said, "You are My Beloved Son, in whom I am well pleased." (Mark 1:11) Jesus had not preached a sermon, healed any sickness, or done anything religious, yet God said, "You are My Beloved Son, and I'm pleased with you."

Jesus began His public ministry in the power of knowing that He was the Father's beloved. This revelation of His Father's love and acceptance empowered Him to overcome the devil in the wilderness.

As recorded in the Gospels, the temptations of Jesus reveal the strategy of the devil. His goal is to get us to not only doubt that we are sons and daughters of God, but also to doubt God's love for us. Satan began his temptation of Jesus with these words: "If you are the Son of God...." I read these verses for years before I saw that satan had left out one word each time. What was it? BELOVED. He didn't say if you are the Beloved Son of God. Why leave that word out? Because satan knows that temptation can only be truly successful to those who doubt God's Love for them. This is why the Apostle Paul prayed often that we would come to the spiritual revelation of God's love for us.

> *may be able to comprehend with all the saints what is the width and length and depth and height –* [19] *to know the love of Christ which passes knowledge; that you may be filled with all the fullness of God.* (Ephesians 3:18-19)

Don't buy into the myth that our greatest need is to love God more. It's not true. We need to go back to the truth in a child's song, "Jesus loves me this I know for the Bible tells me so."

Chapter 13

Myth: God Is Angry with Sinners

On July 8, 1741, Jonathan Edwards preached the most famous sermon ever delivered in the history of America. It was entitled, "Sinners in the Hands of an Angry God." This sermon painted God as full of anger and vengeful toward sinners. Let's read an excerpt from this sermon:

> *The God that holds you over the pit of hell, much as one holds a spider, or some loathsome insect over the fire, abhors you, and is dreadfully provoked: his wrath towards you burns like fire; he looks upon you as worthy of nothing else, but to be cast into the fire; he is of purer eyes than to bear to have you in his sight; you are ten thousand*

times more abominable in his eyes, than the most hateful venomous serpent is in ours.

Is this view of God accurate? Jonathan Edwards said, "God holds you over hell, that He abhors [HATES] you, that His wrath towards you burns like fire." What? Is this the "Father" that Jesus showed us? Absolutely not! Until the incarnation of Christ, no man had ever truly seen or known God. No, not Moses, David, Elijah, or even Jacob. They had caught glimpses of Him, but none of them really knew Him as Father. Remember Phillip asked Jesus to show us the Father. Jesus replied, "He who has seen Me has seen the Father" (John 14:8-9). Jesus paints the Father as anything but angry. According to Jesus, He is a God who does not condemn a woman caught in the very act of adultery (even though she didn't repent or ask for forgiveness). He goes out of His way to converse with sinners, turns water into wine to keep the party going, takes tax collectors as His disciples, and dines with sinners.

Prior to Jesus' coming, there was wrath from God against mankind for its sins. Once the Law was given by Moses, the Old Testament writers recorded a brutal history of God's wrath upon sin and disobedience. But all that changed at the cross of Jesus Christ. Prior to the death of Jesus, people's sins were held against them. But when Jesus died, God stopped holding people's sins against them. This is exactly what the Bible teaches:

*12 For I will be merciful to their unrighteousness, **and their sins and their lawless deeds I will remember no more.**"* (Hebrews 8:12)

*then He adds, **"Their sins and their lawless deeds I will remember no more.**"* (Hebrews 10:17)

Isaiah spoke about this glorious New Covenant that would bring God's anger to an end:

> *⁸ With a little wrath I hid My face from you for a moment; But with **everlasting kindness** I will have mercy on you," Says the LORD, your Redeemer. ⁹ "For this is like the waters of Noah to Me; For as I have sworn That the waters of Noah would no longer cover the earth, So have I sworn That **I would not be angry with you, nor rebuke you.** ¹⁰ For the mountains shall depart And the hills be removed, But My kindness shall not depart from you, Nor shall My covenant of peace be removed," Says the LORD, who has mercy on you.* (Isaiah 54:8-10)

> *¹⁹ that is, that God was in Christ reconciling the world to Himself, **not imputing their trespasses to them**, and has committed to us the word of reconciliation.* (2 Corinthians 5:19)

The word "reconciliation" is talking about making peace. God was no longer holding our sins against us. Instead, He imputed our sins to Jesus, making Jesus accountable for our sins. Thank God for Jesus! This is the reason God is *not* angry with unbelievers. At the cross, more than 2000 years ago, the sin of the whole world was forgiven by God and His Grace was extended to all men.

> *For the Grace of God that brings salvation has appeared to all men.* (Titus 2:11)

However, a person must put their faith in this grace to receive it. God has already reconciled the entire world to Himself through Jesus. God has already allowed all punishment against sin to be poured out on the body of Jesus, and He has also forgiven everybody's sin. But people have to believe in Jesus to receive the benefit of that forgiveness. Because of Jesus, the wrath of God towards sin has been fully satisfied. I'm not saying there are no consequences for sin because there are. It's just not God punishing you.

Nor am I saying all are saved because forgiveness does not equal salvation. Salvation, of course, includes forgiveness of sin, but salvation is much more than mere forgiveness. It is eternal life. Jesus said, "I have come that they might have life" (John 10:10). It was not just that we sinned and needed forgiveness. It was that we were dead and needed life!

Christians have misconceptions about what the Christian life is all about. Many Christians think that when they are going through hard and difficult circumstances that they're being punished by God for some past sins. This way of thinking is so pervasive in the church. Nothing about "punishment" is part of our relationship with God. Jesus took that all away when He was punished for us on the cross. We are always forgiven, continuously, perpetually, and eternally forgiven, and accepted by Him. His death has rendered us un-punishable! (Not un-discipline-able.)

No matter what your preacher tells you, God is not punishing you for your sin, nor is He judging America or any other nation for their sin. I've heard preachers say, "If God doesn't judge America, He will have to apologize to Sodom and Gomorrah." The truth is that if God judges America for her sin, He will have to apologize to Jesus. He would be saying, "Sorry, Son, your sacrifice was not enough. You didn't take away their sin."

Some may be thinking, "What about John 3:36?"

> *He who believes in the Son has everlasting life; and he who does*
> *not believe the Son shall not see life, but the wrath of God abides on*
> *him.* (John 3:36)

What does it mean when John makes the statement that the wrath of God abides on the unbeliever? He means the unbeliever has rejected the free gift of God's love and grace. He's trusting in himself, sowing to the flesh, loving darkness instead of light, and earning the wages of sin. John is not saying that God is angry with that person. The testimony of Paul is that God loves sinners (Romans 5:8). This is the good news of the cross!

There is a coming day of wrath, but it's a single day, a one-time event. On that *one single day* of judgment and not years and years as some say (see Romans 2:5), these unbelievers will be judged for *not* believing in Jesus, and they will have to face the consequences of not *receiving* forgiveness for their sins. God is extending His Grace and Goodness towards everybody on the planet (believers and unbelievers alike) because He wants them to see that He is good and that He loves them. It is the goodness of God that leads people to repentance, not holding people over hell:

> *Or do you despise the riches of His goodness, forbearance, and*
> *longsuffering, not knowing that the goodness of God leads you to*
> *repentance?* (Romans 2:4)

Our job is to show them the love of God, not condemn and judge them. We are to do what 2 Corinthians 5:20 tells us to do: *"We implore you on Christ's behalf, be reconciled to God."* Could it be that God wants us to experience His Love and grace as people that are unpunishable, and then manifest that love and grace toward one another? The sin debt has been paid. That's why Jesus came. He suffered all of God's wrath against all the sin of all of mankind. Those who receive God's grace by accepting salvation as a gift by faith in Jesus no longer have any wrath against them. The Lord will never be angry with us again. **Jesus forever changed the way God relates to mankind**. Hallelujah!

Chapter 14

Myth: If You Don't Pay Your Tithes, You Are Under a Curse from God

Is tithing for today? Is there a biblical case for tithing in the New Covenant? Is the New Testament believer under a curse for not tithing? Do you "pay tithes" like you do a bill? I will deal with this often-misunderstood subject by going to the very heart of tithing.

There is a principle of interpretation of the Bible (Bible hermeneutics) which is called **the law of first mention**. The law of first mention simply means that the very first time any important word is mentioned in the Bible, there we find its most complete, and accurate, meaning to not only serve as a "key" in understanding the word's Biblical concept, but to also provide a foundation for its fuller development in later parts of the Bible. For example, the first time the word "love" appears in the Bible is found in Genesis 22:2, where Abraham is told *to sacrifice Isaac, your only son whom you LOVE.* Therefore, the foundational revelation of love is not the love between a man and a woman, but the love of a father for his son who is to be sacrificed. This is the story of the Bible. The first time the word "tithe" appears in the Bible is found in Genesis 14:17-23:

> *[17] And the king of Sodom went out to meet him at the Valley of Shaveh (that is, the King's Valley), after his return from the defeat of Chedorlaomer and the kings who were with him. [18] Then Melchizedek king of Salem brought out* **bread and wine**; *he was the priest of God Most High.*
>
> *[9] And he blessed him and said: "Blessed be Abram of God Most High, Possessor of heaven and earth; And blessed be God Most High, Who has delivered your enemies into your hand." And he gave him a* **tithe** *of all. [21] Now the king of Sodom said to Abram, "Give me the persons, and take the goods for yourself." [22] But Abram said to the king of Sodom, "I have raised my hand to the LORD, God Most High, the Possessor of heaven and earth, [23] that I will take nothing, from a thread to a sandal strap, and that I will not take anything that is yours, lest you should say, "I have made Abram rich."*

I want you to notice several things in these verses. We have a King/Priest called Melchizedek. He brought out "bread and wine" (Communion) and gave it first to Abram. Then Abram was so moved by this King/Priest that he "gave" (not paid) him a tithe of all.

Who Was This Man Melchizedek?

There are some who debate the identity of this mysterious High Priest who appeared to Abram. I believe that it is absolutely clear from scripture that this man who met Abram was a pre-incarnate appearance of the Lord Jesus Christ. Here is what Hebrews says about this man:

> *¹ For this Melchizedek, king of Salem, priest of the Most High God, who met Abraham returning from the slaughter of the kings and blessed him, ² to whom also Abraham **gave** a tenth part of all, first being translated **"king of righteousness,"** and then also king of Salem, meaning **"king of peace,"** ³ **without father, without mother, without genealogy, having neither beginning of days nor end of life,** but made **like the Son of God,** remains **a priest continually.** ⁴ Now consider how great this man was, to whom even the patriarch Abraham **gave** a tenth of the spoils.* (Hebrews 7:1-4)

No one other than Jesus Christ could meet this description. There are several things to take away from these passages. Giving a tenth declares this man is great. Giving of the tithe is a declaration of the greatness of God. Is there such a thing as giving a tithe under grace? I believe the answer has to be yes because Abram did it, and he preceded the Law by over four hundred years. However, I disagree with the way tithing is taught in most churches.

Debunking Malachi 3:8-12

I know that this teaching will challenge some of the long-held views about how we tithe. Like many of the myths in this book, there was a time I preached this myself. I used these verses in Malachi as the foundation for tithing in my own life and for the members of my church. However, I now believe that the church's use of Malachi 3:8-12 as the biblical basis for tithing is misleading, self-defeating, and manipulative.

I'm not saying that most pastors intentionally try to manipulate their people with these verses. Most are just echoing what they have heard others teach. Some may even be angered by my attempt to divorce the church from this pattern of tithing. I have found that usually the people most concerned over this teaching are the pastors that derive their income from such giving, which is an amazing coincidence. I, too, am supported by the churches giving, but I must be biblically honest as we look at the subject of tithing/giving under grace.

Malachi 3:8-12 is often used as a big stick to cause people to "pay" their tithes and to give out of fear, not faith. It frequently goes something like this: "If you don't pay your tithes, then you're robbing God and you're under a curse and you're opening the door to the devourer." Wow! That's pretty scary stuff.

One of the reasons that many believers struggle to give their tithe consistently is the use of this "curse threat" from the pulpit as pastors endeavor to get their people to give. Most honest students of the Bible know that the problem with this curse teaching is Galatians 3:13 where we are told that *Christ has redeemed us from the curse of the law, having become a curse for us.*

The curse described in Malachi is part of the curse of the Law. So why do preachers continue to tell us we are cursed if we don't pay our tithes? My point exactly. Either we are cursed or the curse has been removed by Christ on the cross. So, which is it? Obviously, you should not fall for this Law-based teaching for we are under grace, not Law.

The prophet Malachi, contrary to many pastors, was not rebuking the children of Israel for not paying their tithes. His target audience was the Levitical priests who were mishandling the Lord's tithes and offerings.

> *And now, **O priests**, this commandment is for you.* (Malachi 2:1)

Malachi wrote to remind the Levitical priesthood to "remember the Law of Moses" (Malachi 4:4). Nothing could be clearer than this. So here is my question. "Are we under the Law of Moses, or are we under grace?" There has been a change of priesthood (Hebrews 7:12). The Levitical priesthood is no longer valid. It was of the Law. Jesus is a priest forever, according to the order of Melchizedek, which is under grace.

The first tithe was given, not paid. Under Levitical priesthood, the tithes were paid and were connected to services rendered.

> *Behold, I have given the children of Levi all the tithes in Israel as an inheritance in return for the work which they perform, the work of the tabernacle of meeting.* (Numbers 18:21)

This mentality is still prevalent in the church today. One of the first things the average Christian will do when they dislike something at their church is withhold the tithe. Under grace, the tithe is giving.

Let's look at the differences in these two priesthoods.

Levitical (LAW)	Melchizedek (GRACE)
Tithe is paid	Tithe is given
Motivation is fear of curse	Motivation is honor
Temporary priesthood	Eternal priesthood
Continual sacrifice for sin	One sacrifice for sin, for all
Sin covered and remembered	Sin removed and forgotten
Eat fruit from the ground	Fed heavenly bread and wine
No power to rebuke the devourer	Power to rebuke the devourer
Open window	Open door
Only Levites in ministry	Everyone in the ministry of reconciliation
Priest only	King, Priest, and Prophet
Veil that separates	No veil to separate you any longer
Relationship based on Law	Relationship based on Son of God
Priest never sits, never finished	Jesus is seated, He is finished
Couldn't make perfect	Perfected forever

The coming of our Great High Priest Melchizedek (Jesus Christ) changed everything. I've heard ministers proclaim the blessings of tithing according to the Malachi 3 passages, but the blessings of the Order of Melchizedek far surpass all the Levitical blessings. I hear great emphasis placed on God opening the windows of heaven and pouring out blessings for you. Let me ask you a question. If I must open a window at my house and pour out to you a glass of water, where are you? You are outside the house, not in the house. Paul said that before we were saved, we were *outside the commonwealth of Israel and strangers from the covenants of promise, having no hope and without God in the world* (Ephesians 2:12).

Would you rather have an "open window" and be outside the house (blessings), or would you rather come through the "open door" (Jesus Christ) and be seated inside the house with Christ in heavenly places? Would you rather have no power to rebuke with authority the devourer, or would you like to have the gift of authority over the devourer? Do you want some blessings or **the** blessing?

Melchizedek (Jesus) shows up unexpectedly to Abram who is returning from a victorious battle, and He does an amazing thing – He serves communion. Remember, this was before Passover and the cross. Melchizedek appears with bread and wine, saying, "Let's give praise and thanks to God." Why? Because Abram was told that the reason he experienced this extraordinary victory was because of God's blessings on his life. Abram has just had an encounter with grace. What is his response? He gives a tenth of all he has. Abram's giving of the tithe was not a Law requirement, but rather an acknowledgement of Christ's Lordship over his life. It was recognition that he owed his victory in battle to God Most High, and the tithe he gave was the response of an inspired, grateful heart.

In Genesis 14, we have here not only the word "tithe", but also bread and wine which are the elements of communion. Do we practice bread and wine today under grace? YES. Is Abraham our Father, father of faith? Daniel is not our father. Moses is not our father, but Abraham is.

So then those who are of faith are blessed with believing Abraham. (Galatians 3:9)

When we keep the communion (bread and wine), we are remembering and proclaiming the Lord's death. But when we give the tithe, we are proclaiming that He lives. Our giving of the tithe is a witness that He lives.

*Here mortal men receive tithes, but there he receives them, of whom **it is witnessed that he lives**.* (Hebrews 7:8)

Here, on earth, men receive tithes, but there, in heaven, He receives them. Verse eight says, He receives tithes. Would Jesus receive anything that He is not supposed to receive? The fact that He receives them is proof that we should give them. Today we tithe and give out of revelation, not obligation. I guess one question we need to answer is "Does the tithe still belong to the Lord?" Let me ask this, "Does honor still belong to God?" Yes. Then we should give unto the Lord the honor that is due Him. And, if the tithe belongs to the Lord and not us, we should still honor the Lord with His tithe. There is nothing more powerful and life giving than the bestowment of honor upon whom honor is due. Today we are suffering from the lost culture of honor. Honor has fallen on hard times in our society. Independence is championed. No spiritual culture can ever be referred to as a kingdom culture that does not have this principle of honor deeply imbedded in it.

Honor the Lord with your possessions, And with the first fruits of all your increase; So your barns will be filled with plenty, And your vats will overflow with new wine. (Proverbs 3:9, 10)

In the above verse, we are told how to honor the Lord, "with your possessions, with the first fruits of all your increase". What is the result of honoring the Lord with your possessions? Your barns will be filled with plenty and your vats will overflow with new wine. Honor releases life on any area on which it is bestowed. Some people may say there's not enough New Testament evidence that tells us to tithe. My answer to that statement is that there's not enough New Testament evidence that tells us **not** to tithe. I don't have enough faith to stop tithing because there's not enough scriptural evidence to show me that the tithe doesn't belong to God anymore. The account of Abram tithing to Melchizedek is very important. It has absolute significance to New Covenant believers, as Christ is a high priest in the order of Melchizedek. The fact that Melchizedek blessed Abraham before he tithed is a picture of grace. That shows us that he wasn't motivated to tithe because he was looking for blessings. Under grace, our tithing doesn't earn God's blessings because He has blessed us with every spiritual blessing in the heavenly places in Christ (Ephesians 1:3). The blessing came to Abraham through the Grace of God, displayed in the bread and the wine, which for us is through the finished work of Jesus! The Levitical priesthood received tithes to show that tithing was under the Law, and the Melchizedek priesthood also received tithes to show that tithing is under grace. I will end this chapter with this instruction from the Apostle Paul:

> *⁶ Remember this: Whoever sows sparingly will also reap sparingly, and whoever sows generously will also reap generously. ⁷ Each man should give what he has decided in his heart to give, not reluctantly or under compulsion, for God loves a cheerful giver. ⁸ And God is able to make all grace abound to you, so that in all things at all times, having all that you need, you will abound in every good work. ⁹ As it is written: "He has scattered abroad his gifts to the poor; his righteousness endures forever." ¹⁰ Now he who supplies seed to the*

sower and bread for food will also supply and increase your store of seed and will enlarge the harvest of your righteousness. [11] You will be made rich in every way so that you can be generous on every occasion, and through us your generosity will result in thanksgiving to God. (2 Corinthians 9:6-11 NIV)

Chapter 15

Myth: Hyper-Grace Is Dangerous

Hyper-grace, according to some in the church world, is a dangerous and unbiblical teaching. They say that preachers that preach God's grace as "hyper" have taken grace too far. The accusation that hyper or extreme grace is unbiblical is easy to test. All you need is a Bible.

*[20] Moreover the law entered that the offense might abound. But where sin abounded, **grace abounded much more**.* (Romans 5:20)

*[20] But then Law came in, [only] to expand and increase the trespass [making it more apparent and exciting opposition]. But where sin increased and abounded, grace (God's unmerited favor) has surpassed it and increased the more **and superabounded**.* (Romans 5:20 AMP)

Paul's use of the words "abounded much more" and "superabounded" is where the term "hyper-grace" originates. Most of the time when you hear the term hyper-grace, it is usually used in a negative way. Like "be careful of those hyper-grace preachers." What we need to fear is those "hypo-grace" preachers, those who diminish and dilute God's grace by mixing it with Law. Paul says, where sin abounded (pleonazo), grace did much more abound (huper-perisseuo). The prefix huper or hyper is like the Latin "super." So, where sin could be measured or counted, grace could never be measured or counted. Our text might well read, "Where sin was finite, grace was infinite."

To suggest that God's grace is anything less than hyper is unbiblical and blasphemous. It's like saying God is good but He's not that good. He's holy but not that holy. When you diminish grace, you diminish God. I don't hear anybody complaining about hyper-love or hyper-forgiveness? Some preachers are afraid of grace because they think it encourages sin. If Jesus paid it all and it is finished, if the judgment against us has been fully paid by Jesus Christ on the cross, aren't we opening the door to sin? This is exactly what the Judiaziers were afraid of. They didn't like the Gospel of hyper-grace because they thought people would get out of control. If God is not mad at me and if he will never love me more than he does right now, then why can't I sin like crazy? The point is that you can sin if you want to, but the reality is that once you've met grace, you won't desire to sin.

Although the term grace is often spoken in the church, there is much confusion of what grace actually is. In more than two decades of attending church, I never heard one message about the Grace of God. When I did hear grace mentioned, it was usually negative.

Terms like greasy grace and cheap grace were used to warn us of the dangers of hyper-grace. I admit that some think grace is their "get out of jail free card." They don't know what grace is. They have a concept, but they don't have grace.

Grace is a Person living His life through you. Grace has eyes (Genesis 6:8). Grace is not a theology. It is not another subject in the Bible. Grace is the subject of the Bible. It is not a doctrine. It is a Person, and His name is Jesus. That's the reason the Lord wants you to receive the abundance of grace – because to have the abundance of grace is to have the abundance of Jesus.

I find it confusing that those who believe in the forgiveness of sins past, present, and future (by the way, Billy Graham believes this) are disparagingly labeled as being HYPER-GRACE.

Well, can't grace be abused? Yes, but love can be abused; forgiveness can be abused. Isn't this the point though? If it can't be abused, then it's not really grace at all! Does this mean that you can go out and sin without fear of judgment because you are in Christ? Yes, you can, but that doesn't mean that there aren't consequences to continuing to sin. For example, if I foolishly decide to rob a bank, I will soon find myself in jail! That doesn't mean that God is paying me back or judging me for my sin of stealing. Of course, even in our stupidity, God's Grace abounds, and grace will teach you, even in a jail cell, that continuing to sin is a dumb idea! By the way, what's the real difference? If every sin you commit today must be individually confessed and repented of in order to be forgiven, then you can still go out and sin, repent, confess and get God's forgiveness anyway – because you know the outcome. You know God's heart is to forgive!

While attacks on morality will always come from outside the church, attacks on grace will always come from inside the church. If you want to make people mad, preach the Law. If you want to make people really mad, preach grace. Grace is scandalous. It's hard to accept, hard to believe, and hard to receive. Why? Because grace shocks us in what it offers. It's too good to be true, yet it is. That's why it's grace.

You don't deserve it. It is truly not of this world. It frightens us with what it does for sinners. Grace shows us that God does for others what we would never do for them. We would save the "not so bad," but God gives grace to prostitutes and forgives those who don't even ask for forgiveness. Grace is a gift that costs everything to the giver and nothing to the receiver. It is given to those who don't deserve it, don't ask for it, barely recognize it, and don't appreciate it. That's why God alone gets the glory in your salvation. You are saved by grace through faith in God's Son and His Goodness. Jesus did all the work when He died on the cross.

The Law added transgressions, showing even more clearly the hyper-Grace of God. Grace did not set aside the Law, but rather completely satisfied it. As deep as sin goes, God's grace goes deeper. When sin abounded, grace super-abounded. God's grace is greater than all our sin. Why is it so easy for people to believe that they were condemned and made sinners because of Adam's sin, but they find it so hard to believe that they have been made righteous by Jesus' sacrifice on the cross?

This is the reason the devil hates the message of grace and fights it so hard – because God's Grace is the only antidote for sin. It is the only solution to man's problem, the only cure for man's disease. Grace is so wonderful because like medicine it stops the infection.

It breaks into the sin/confess/sin cycle. (The sin/confess cycle is exactly what Roman Catholics practice in the confession booth and Protestants do privately and every Sunday.) However, none of this religious performance results in deliverance or righteousness, just frustration, sometimes desperation – and many just give up, give in, and continue to sin. The Law offends us because it tells us what to do, and we hate anyone telling us what to do. But grace offends us even more because it tells us that there's nothing we can do, that everything has already been done. And if there's something we hate more than being told what to do, it's being told that we can't do anything, that we can't earn anything, and that we're helpless, weak, and needy.

Grace is not "fair". We can't understand how a prodigal son can return home after blowing all his inheritance on wine, women, and song, and receive grace. It looks to us like he's rewarded for his bad behavior. He is not punished or rebuked by his father. In fact, just the opposite. He is given the best clothes, a ring, and shoes, and thrown a party. Now that's "hyper-grace"! Grace is counter-intuitive. It turns everything that makes sense to us upside-down. It's not rational. It offends our deepest sense of justice and rightness.

It doesn't surprise me at all when I hear people react negatively to grace. It doesn't surprise me that the religious warn us of hyper-grace. That's just religion that loves rules. By nature, people are addicted to a legalistic method of salvation. Even after you become a Christian by believing the Gospel, your heart is still addicted to salvation by works. You find it hard to believe that you should get any blessing before you work for it. The religious flesh is always resistant to "It is finished".

The negative use of the term hyper-grace is ridiculous. You need not fear that you carry grace too far. Most people haven't gone far enough in their revelation of grace. I thank God for His hyper, amazing, super, lavish, and scandalous grace. God's Grace has appeared to all men. **The only restriction is that it must be** *accepted***; it has to be** *received* **by faith.** The only way you can miss the Grace of God is if you reject it!

Chapter 16

Myth: You Need to Try and Please God

In almost thirty years of pastoring, I've heard this myth many times. Christians say to me, "I just want to please God. I've been praying more and reading my Bible more." I have asked congregations this question, "How many of you want to please God?" Every hand will go up saying yes. But then I ask them, "How many of you feel that you are pleasing God right now?" and hardly any hands will go up. I have asked Christians who were struggling with trying to please God, "On a scale of 1 to 10, how do you think you're doing?" The highest number any believer has ever given me is a 6. This is a huge problem. We desire to please God, yet we feel that we are failing. Just search Google on the topic of pleasing God, and you will find teachings like "7 ways to please God," "13 ways to please God." I even saw one (no kidding) that said "50 ways to please God"! If you don't do all 7 or 13 or 50, is God not pleased with us?

The problem is that our question is wrong. Today, you should no longer be asking yourself, "Am I pleasing God?" This question puts the focus back on you, and this places you under the Law. When you were born again, you were taken out of Adam and placed in Christ. *"If any man be in Christ, he is a new creation"* (2 Corinthians 5:17). The correct question to ask is "Is God pleased with Christ?" Then He is pleased with you. Can you see the difference in emphasis? The Old Covenant of Law is all about you, but the New Covenant of grace is all about Jesus! The Law places the demand on you to perform and makes you self-conscious, whereas grace places the demand on Jesus and makes you Christ-conscious.

Jesus came to the Jordan where His relative John was baptizing and asked John to baptize Him. The only reason John complied, even though he felt Jesus should be baptizing *him* instead, was because Jesus told him it was "fitting for us to fulfill all righteousness." After John baptized Jesus, His Father spoke with a *voice out of the heavens and said, "This is My beloved Son, in whom I am well-pleased"* (Matthew 3:17). The timing of the Father's words is very significant. Remember this was on the eve of Jesus' public ministry! Up to this point, Jesus hadn't performed a single miracle, hadn't healed anyone, hadn't taught, or preached a sermon, and all still knew Him as "the carpenter," yet the Father Himself said He was well-pleased with His Son. Jesus hadn't successfully resisted the devil; yet the Father opened the heavens and said He was pleased. We need to know that our heavenly Father is pleased with us as well. Before we did anything **religious**, our Father was pleased with us.

Walk up to someone and say, "I please God," and see what kind of response you receive. The response from most people will be something like this: "Who are you to say that you please God? Who do you think you are?" Their reaction will let you know immediately if they are religious or have a real relationship with God.

> *⁵ By faith Enoch was taken away so that he did not see death, "and was not found, because God had taken him"; for before he was taken* **he had this testimony, that he pleased God.** *⁶ But without faith it is impossible to please Him, for he who comes to God must believe that He is, and that He is a rewarder of those who diligently seek Him.* (Hebrews 11:5-6)

Enoch was translated because he was willing to say that he pleased God. It was his testimony that "I please God." Enoch didn't have the new birth experience. He was in faith looking forward to the day that Jesus would come. He was like Abraham who saw Jesus' day and was glad (John 8:56).

What is the requirement to please God? One thing – faith! Faith is what pleases God and without faith, it is impossible to please Him. If an Old Covenant person who was not even born again could please God, how much more can we in the New Covenant of God's grace? When you place your faith in Jesus Christ, you are born again. You are a new creation (2 Corinthians 5:17). You have been placed in Christ. Is God pleased with Jesus? Yes! Then God is pleased with you. We struggle with this thought that we please God because we don't know what is new.

> *Therefore, if anyone is in Christ, he is a new creation; old things have passed away; behold, all things have become new.* (2 Corinthians 5:17)

What does that mean? It must be talking about our spirit man. The new you is truly new. The new you still has your old mind and the same body, but your spirit is brand new. The key to victorious living as a believer is learning to live from the new born-again spirit instead of the old man.

> [23] *and be renewed in the spirit of your mind,* [24] *and that **you put on the new man which <u>was created</u> according to God, in true righteousness and holiness.** (Ephesians 4:23-24)

Notice verse 24 says your new man **was** created that way, not will be created some day. When was your spirit created in true righteousness and holiness? When you were born again. It is not a process of you performing or doing things to become that way. You were made (born again) that way. You do not grow in righteousness. Righteousness is a gift (Romans 5:17-18). You do not grow in holiness. You were created in holiness when you accepted Christ. Now that's Good News! Look at these verses in Hebrews.

> [14] *For by one offering **He has perfected forever** those who are being sanctified.* (Hebrews 10:14)

> [23] *to the general assembly and church of the firstborn who are registered in heaven, to God the Judge of all, **to the spirits of just men made perfect,** (Hebrews 12:23)

Your spirit has been perfected forever. Your spirit is perfect! That's not what the church and religion would have you believe, but that's what the Bible declares. In your spirit, you are righteous, holy, and perfect!

*¹⁷ Love has been perfected among us in this: that we may have boldness in the day of judgment; **because as He is, so are we in this world**.* (1 John 4:17)

What does this mean? In our born-again spirit, we are identical to Jesus. As He is. Is Jesus holy, righteous, and perfect? Yes! Then so are we in this world. Not we will be in the next world, but right now in your spirit, you are just like Jesus! Learn to live out of this revelation. Be led by your spirit and not by your flesh. God is Spirit. He relates Spirit to spirit, not Spirit to your flesh. God sees you as you are in your spirit. He relates to you as you are in your spirit, not based on your actions or performance. Man looks at your outward self, your actions, your deeds, and judges you by them, but God looks on the inward man, on who you are in the spirit (1 Samuel 16:7). God does not relate to you based on your sin but on His Son; not on your obedience, but on His Obedience; not on your righteousness, but on His Righteousness.

I'm not saying sin doesn't matter or that sin does not hurt, because it does. I'm not making little of sin, but much of Jesus. You've probably heard it said that there is not anything that you can do to make God love you more or anything that you can do to make Him love you less. This is true. God didn't start loving you when you received Christ as your savior. *"While we were sinners God demonstrated His love for us."* (Romans 5:8) Not even my sins and my actions will change God's heart toward me, but my sins will affect my heart toward God. My sins will not cause Him to love me less, but my sins will cause me to love Him less.

Be like Enoch. Have as your testimony that you please God, and you also will be "translated" to live a life led by the spirit, a life of victory! Know that you are also His beloved son or daughter, in whom He is well pleased.

Chapter 17

Myth: The Holy Spirit Convicts Believers of Their Sins

Does the Bible really teach that the Holy Spirit convicts us of our sins? Does He convict the unbeliever of their sins? Like most believers, I was taught this myth. I was also taught to pray for unbelievers like this: "Lord, I pray that the Holy Spirit will convict them of their sins, that He will bring them under conviction." The motive was good, but it was a pointless prayer to ask Him to convict them of the sins that they were doing. Why? Because their sins are not their main problem. Their sins and the sins of the world were taken away by Jesus Christ on the cross. Their sins are simply a symptom of their deeper problem, and that is their unbelief in Jesus.

Our view of the Holy Spirit, like our view of God, needs adjustment. I was taught that the Holy Spirit was like a dove and that He was easily offended and would leave. I was taught that if I did the wrong thing He would leave, that He was hard to get to come and easy to run off. That's why we sang songs like "Come Holy Spirit," because we lacked the revelation that He was in us and that He would never leave us. Many get confused. They pray Old Testament prayers like David did in Psalm 51:11. *"Do not cast me away from Your presence, And do not take Your Holy Spirit from me."* That was appropriate for David at the time, but it's wrong for us today.

We have too many New Testaments saints with Old Testament minds. We pray that God will send His Holy Spirit. He already did. We pray and ask God to pour out His Spirit. He already has. In Acts, chapter 2, the Holy Spirit came rushing in like a mighty wind. Yet some say they had to "tarry" for ten days before He came. People again get a messed-up theology because they are ignorant of the Feast Days. The Holy Spirit was not waiting on them to pray enough, get in unity, or any of the other things I've heard preached. He was simply waiting for the Day of Pentecost to arrive. He is here, in you and for you. You don't have to beg Him to come. He is our helper, our guide, the Spirit of Truth, and the Spirit of Grace.

There is only one verse in the New Testament linking the Holy Spirit with the conviction of sin.

> [7] *Nevertheless I tell you the truth. It is to your advantage that I go away; for if I do not go away, the Helper will not come to you; but if*

I depart, I will send Him to you. ⁸ And when He has come, He will **convict the world of sin,** *and of righteousness, and of judgment:* ⁹ *of sin,* **because <u>they</u> do not believe in Me;** ¹⁰ *of righteousness, because I go to My Father and you see Me no more;* ¹¹ *of judgment, because the ruler of this world is judged.* ¹² *I still have many things to say to you, but you cannot bear them now.* (John 16:7-12)

The word "convict" here does not mean that He finds you guilty. The Greek word used here is also the word that means "to convince". He will convince the unbeliever of his unbelief in Jesus. Notice the word "they" in verse nine. These are the unbelievers. The Holy Spirit is not nagging believers and pointing at you when you do wrong. Many believers say, "The Holy Spirit convicted me of my sin." How can He convict you of what He no longer remembers? The Holy Spirit is God.

For I will be merciful to their unrighteousness, and their sins and their lawless deeds I will remember no more. (Hebrews 8:12)

Why did the same Holy Spirit then inspire Paul to write *"that love keeps no record of wrongs"* (1Corinthians 13:5)? Why would the Holy Spirit remind you of a sin that Jesus took away? Jesus removed our sin as far as the east is from the west. Do we really believe that the Father says, "I will remember their sins no more" but the Holy Spirit says to the Father, "Don't worry, I will remind you of their sins"? Can we not see how foolish this is?

Jesus said that the Holy Spirit does three things. First, He convinces the unbeliever of his unbelief because that is his problem. His doing drugs, getting drunk, and whatever other sins he commits are just symptoms of his unbelief and distrust in Jesus. Second, He convinces the one that believes of his righteousness. He convinces you that you are the righteousness of God in Christ. Why is it so important to be convinced that you are righteous by faith? Because when a person can believe that they are made righteous now by faith, then all these other things will be added to them (Matthew 6:33). If you can have faith and believe that you are righteous by just believing, then you have the faith to be healed and to receive His blessings. Third, He convinces us that the devil is judged, not you. God is not judging you for your sin. Jesus has already suffered the judgment for sin.

> [24] *Most assuredly, I say to you, he who hears My word and believes in Him who sent Me has everlasting life, **and shall not come into judgment**, but has passed from death into life.* (John 5:24)

Those that are in Christ have no condemnation or judgment in their future. Jesus bore their sins and punishment in His own body on the cross. If Jesus has already received our judgment for our sin, then God would be unjust to punish two different people for the same sin. I didn't say that God doesn't care if you sin and that there are no consequences to your sin. I'm just saying don't blame God. He's not punishing you.

You may say, "Well, if the Holy Spirit isn't convicting me, what is?" Your own conscience.

> *Then those who heard it, being **convicted by their conscience**, went out one by one, beginning with the oldest even to the last. And Jesus was left alone, and the woman standing in the midst.* (John 8:9)

It is your conscience that is condemning you, not God. That is not the work of the Holy Spirit. The Holy Spirit is never the source of any of your guilt or condemnation. He is not the one who makes you feel bad when you sin.

For if our heart condemns us, God is greater than our heart, and knows all things. (1 John 3:20)

This verse is clear. It is our own heart that condemns us, not the Holy Spirit. Jesus called the Holy Spirit the "Comforter", not the judge. The Holy Spirit doesn't convict the world of lying, stealing, adultery, or murder. He convicts them of not trusting in Jesus. That's the root of every sin. Even after receiving salvation, it's not our actions (sins) that are the problem but the heart attitude of not trusting Jesus. We don't seem to understand that God desires more than just obedience. You can obey someone that you don't necessarily trust. You obey the flight attendant, but you're probably not going to leave your wallet with her. The reason we sin is, at least in that moment, that we are not trusting God, but we turn to something other than Jesus to comfort us.

Most Christians have thought that the Holy Spirit was the source of their feelings of guilt, and condemnation, and because of that, they haven't enjoyed the benefits of a real relationship with Him. The Holy Spirit was sent here to encourage you, comfort you, and convince you that you are righteous now in Christ. He wants you to know that your sins are forgiven and that you should live your life out of the fullness of His indwelling presence.

Chapter 18

Myth: You're Out of Fellowship with God When You Sin

I hear this myth said often among Christians. They say, "You're out of fellowship with God because you have committed a sin." What does that mean? Let's first define the word "fellowship". It is the Greek word "koinonia". It means partnership, participation, and communion. It also means oneness and closeness. Paul the Apostle uses this word in describing our relationship to Jesus.

> *God is faithful, by whom you were called into the fellowship of His Son, Jesus Christ our Lord.* (1 Corinthians 1:9)

If you are in Christ, then you are now and forever in fellowship with Him and nothing can change that. Why? Because God is faithful, even when we're not. God called you into this oneness with

Christ. Fellowship is not about how you feel, but about our faith in His Blood. The closeness you have with God is not determined by your behavior but by His Grace. When you were born again, God placed you in Christ. *If anyone is in Christ, he is a new creation* (2 Corinthians 5:17). If you are "in Christ," how can you be out of closeness with Him? That's like saying, "I'm not close to this building," when you are standing inside the building. That doesn't make sense.

I would go to church as a young Christian and often hear the admonition from the leaders to "draw near to God." They would affirm God's promise that "if we would draw near to God, He would draw near to us." You might say, "What's wrong with that? Isn't that in the Bible?" Yes, it's in James, but the problem is that's not the whole verse. Let's read it:

> *Draw near to God and He will draw near to you.* ***Cleanse your hands, you sinners;*** *and purify your hearts, you double-minded.* (James 4:8)

James is writing to sinners, not to born-again believers. He is telling those who are not saved that if they will draw near to God, He will draw near to them and cleanse them. Nowhere in scripture are saints called sinners or sinners called saints.

> [12] *that at that time* ***you were without Christ,*** *being aliens from the commonwealth of Israel and strangers from the covenants of promise, having no hope and without God in the world.*

> [13] ***But now in Christ*** *Jesus you who* ***once were far off*** *have been* ***brought near by the blood*** *of Christ.* (Ephesians 2:12-13)

Do you see it? When you were without Christ, you were far off, but now, you have been brought near/close by the blood of Jesus! What is it that brought you near? Not your performance, your efforts, or your works. It was the blood of Jesus. The distance and barriers that once separated you from God have been removed in Christ. You have been made nigh, by His Blood, and there is nothing that can ever make you "un-nigh" again. If your sin can take you out of fellowship with God, then you're saying that your sin is more powerful than His Blood.

As I have stated in other chapters in this book, I'm not saying that sinning by a Christian is not a big deal. I'm not saying that it's okay to sin. I'm not saying that there are no consequences to sin. I'm simply saying that your sin is not stronger than the blood of Jesus, and it cannot take you out of fellowship with God.

You are in constant fellowship with God through Christ. You may not feel like you are, but your feelings are not true. The word of God is true. The myth that you, as a believer, can ever be out of fellowship with God is a lie. Don't believe it.

> *But if we walk in the light as He is in the light, we have fellowship with one another, and the blood of Jesus Christ His Son cleanses us from all sin.* (1 John 1:7)

Chapter 19

Myth: Your Heart Is Desperately Wicked

Have you ever believed that at your very core you are still wicked, that even though you are a Christian, your heart is sick and sinfully dark? I have, and I got that belief from church. I grew up in church hearing this statement made often in sermons, that our hearts were wicked and not to be trusted, even as a born-again believer. This is a myth. Your heart is no longer untrustworthy and wicked if you've been born again.

Where does the idea that Christians' hearts are desperately wicked come from? It comes from an Old Testament passage of Scripture from Jeremiah 17:9. The most well-known wording is in the KJV: *"The heart is deceitful above all things, and desperately wicked:*

who can know it?" The prophet Jeremiah spoke these words to people living under the Old Covenant Law. This, of course, is before Jesus went to the cross, and this was appropriate and applicable to their hearts' condition. Once sin entered in, the hearts of all men were desperately wicked, sick, depraved, and hopeless. Jeremiah also writes about the depravity of the unbeliever's heart in Jeremiah.

> 13:23 (*Can the Ethiopian change his skin or the leopard its spots? Then may you also do good who are accustomed to do evil.* (Jeremiah 13:23)

He clearly shows us that there is nothing but wickedness and deceit in the unbeliever's heart and that the condition of the wicked person's heart is incurable. But how could anyone dare say that any of these verses are describing our hearts after we have been born again?

The moment we receive the Truth of the Gospel of Jesus Christ, God gives a new heart, and that old heart of stone is removed. Yet some Christians see it as humility to say that one's own heart is still deceitful and desperately wicked. But here is what God says about the heart of the believer:

> [26] *I will give you a new heart and put a new spirit within you; I will take the heart of stone out of your flesh and give you a heart of flesh.* [27] *I will put My Spirit within you and cause you to walk in My statutes, and you will keep My judgments and do them.* (Ezekiel 36:26-27)

That *deceitful* and *incurable heart* is that *stony heart* that is *taken away* and is *replaced* by a *heart of flesh!* The Holy Spirit gives His people a NEW HEART and causes them to walk in His statutes. What does that mean? Our hearts will want what He wants. We will not just be trying to keep the rules. And not only is the heart new, everything is new. You are a NEW CREATION.

> *¹⁷ Therefore, if anyone is in Christ, he is a new creation; old things have passed away; behold, all things have become new.* (2 Corinthians 5:17)

The *old things* include the *old heart.* It is GONE. A great change has taken place! To say that the heart of a believer remains deceitful and incurably wicked is to deny the transforming work of the Lord Jesus Christ and the finished work of the cross!

It is important that you know that you have been given a new heart. Your beliefs govern your behavior. A person's behavior will never change until his/her belief system changes. If you believe at your core that you are still somehow wicked and depraved in your heart, your actions and life will ultimately reflect that. However, if you believe that you have received a new heart, your actions and life will ultimately reflect that too.

Right believing leads to right living.

Chapter 20

Myth: God Writes the Ten Commandments on Our Heart

There are those who teach that New Testament believers must keep the Ten Commandments and, in fact, that God writes those commandments on our hearts. They quote the following:

> *This is the covenant that I will make with them after those days, says the LORD: I will put My laws into their hearts, and in their minds I will write them,* (Hebrews 10:16)

What laws was God referring to when He said, "I will put My **laws** in their mind and write them on their hearts"? He was certainly not referring to the Ten Commandments, known as the Law of the Old Covenant, since He said that He found fault with that covenant and declared it obsolete (Hebrews 8:7,13). The writer of Hebrews is quoting Jeremiah 31:33.

I would also point out that the writer (under the inspiration of the Holy Spirit) changed the "Law" in Jeremiah to "laws" (plural) in Hebrews. He is not referring to the Law but to laws of this New Covenant. Why would God insult His Son's sacrifice by giving you the very thing His sacrifice rendered obsolete? If God wrote the Ten Commandments on our hearts, then Jesus died for nothing.

Let's look at the very next verse after God says, "I will put My laws in their hearts":

> then He adds, *"Their sins and their lawless deeds I will remember no more."* (Hebrews 10:17)

The old Law-keeping covenant required a remembrance of sin, but the New Covenant is characterized by God forgiving and forgetting sin because of Jesus. Why would God do anything to make you fall from grace?

> *You have become estranged from Christ, you who attempt to be justified by law; you have fallen from grace* (Galatians 5:4).

What laws was God referring to then? The laws that God puts in our minds and writes on our hearts refer to **the royal law of love** (Matthew 22:37–40), **the law of liberty** (James 1:22), and **the law of the Spirit of life**. (Romans 8:2) These are the laws of the New Covenant.

> *A new commandment I give you: Love one another. As I have loved you, so you must love one another.* (John 13:34)

Under the old Law covenant, love was demanded from you. "Love the Lord your God with all your heart, soul, mind and strength." But under the New Covenant of grace, love is given to you – "As I have loved you" – and out of the overflow of Christ's measureless love we are able to love others.

How does it happen? *"God's love has been poured out into our hearts through the Holy Spirit, who has been given to us"* (Romans 5:5). You live according to the laws of the New Covenant when you are conscious of God's love for you. This is what fills your heart with love. *"We love Him because He first loved us"* (1 John 4:19).

First, this tells me that we are unable to love properly until we receive the revelation of how much God loves us. The result will be that you will love God and the people around you. That is God writing on your heart the royal law of love.

Second, when you know that you are perfectly accepted by God because of Jesus' sacrifice, you can have the liberty as a child of God to come boldly into the throne of His Grace. The law of liberty describes the finished work of Jesus, and whoever looks intently unto this perfect law will be blessed, for this law declares you righteous in Him.

This is the law of the Spirit of life in Christ. The old law ministered condemnation and death (2 Corinthians 3:7-9), but the new *"law of the Spirit gives life"* (Romans 8:2). *"For the letter kills, but the Spirit gives life"* (2 Corinthians 3:6). What gives life? Jesus does, not a set of rules, but the Spirit of Christ within you. The new law is a Person.

God promised that this New Covenant would come with new laws written upon our hearts. Jeremiah prophesied that those who had the new laws written on their hearts would know the Lord and would no longer need others to teach them.

> *[33] But this is the covenant that I will make with the house of Israel after those days, says the LORD: I will put My law in their minds, and write it on their hearts; and I will be their God, and they shall be My people. [34] No more shall every man teach his neighbor, and every man his brother, saying, 'Know the LORD,' for they all shall know Me, from the least of them to the greatest of them, says the LORD. For I will forgive their iniquity, and their sin I will remember no more.* (Jeremiah 31:33-34)

That which was prophesied in the Old Covenant is now realized in Christ. This is describing that our hearts will want what He wants, that no longer will we need an outside law saying no to sin for us. God's grace teaches us to say no from inside our hearts (Titus 2:11-12). In the Old Testament, the Law said NO for you – "you shall not, you shall not" – but in the New Covenant, grace teaches US to say no. It's not a law saying no; it's us saying no from within. We've been changed now, so we say no. It's not that we really want to say yes, but I "have to say no." We want to say no to sin because that's not who we are any longer. "No" must come from the heart. Christ now lives in you. He is the new law written, by God, in your heart and mind.

Chapter 21

Myth: Sin Is an Action, Something We Do

Jesus did not die for your sins. He died for sin. Sin not sins! With that statement, you are either rejoicing, shocked, or confused. In the KJV of the Bible, the word "sin" is mentioned forty-five times in the book of Romans, and forty-four of those times, it is a noun. Only once is it a verb. The way sin is used in sermons and in conversations, most people have come to perceive the word "sin" only as an action, something we do. Thus, when we read it in our Bibles, we commonly perceive it as a verb. Why is this important? Because if one interprets the word "sin" in Romans as a verb, we will never understand what this book says about sin, which is so vital to us walking in victory.

The first-time sin appears in scripture in Genesis 4:7 (KJV), it is not a verb, but a noun. God says to Cain, *"If thou doest well, shalt thou not be accepted? and if thou doest not well, sin lieth at the door. And unto thee shall be his desire, and thou shalt rule over him."*

God personifies sin. He uses sin as a noun, not a verb. Our theology can be characterized by our definition and our conception of sin. Paul said in Romans 6:14, *"For **sin** shall not have dominion over you: for you are not under the law, but under grace."* The word that Paul used here for sin is a noun. (People, place, or thing) A verb, on the other hand, is a word that describes action. When we think of sin, how many of us think of it as a verb? Doing something wrong! Before Jesus died on the cross, all people were under the bondage and captivity of sin (noun), whether they personally sinned (verb) or not. Sin held all mankind under its captivity because of what Adam did. We were born in a prison called sin and could not get out. In this prison of sin, it didn't matter how many good deeds a person did; he couldn't get out. Adam's sin made all men sinners (Romans 5:19). These people were not sinners because they sinned. They sinned because they were sinners.

It is so important for us to understand complete and total forgiveness of sin. When John the Baptist saw Jesus, he said, *"Behold the Lamb of God that takes away the **SIN** [not sins] of the world"* (John 1:29). Did He take away sin or not? Did He take away just the sin of Christians or did He take away the sin of the world as John said? When forgiveness is taught the way the Bible explains it, people have objections. They question and say, "Doesn't sin matter?"

It's not about your sin.

I know this is hard for some to process and most to accept. We have been raised to beware of sin, to resist sin, to run from sin, to focus on sin, and to try and overcome sin. We have an unhealthy obsession with sin. It is no wonder so many of us are more sin-conscious than we are Christ-conscious. When I didn't understand that Jesus took away SIN, I never really had confidence in my relationship with God. When I felt unworthy because of my failures, instead of turning to God for strength, I would distance myself from Him out of shame, guilt, and fear. My wrong perception was that God was disappointed with me because of my sin. I didn't know that my "sin account" had a ZERO balance. There was no sin in my account!

> *that God was in Christ reconciling the world to Himself,* **not imputing** *their trespasses to them, and has committed to us the word of reconciliation.* (2 Corinthians 5:19)

Most of the church gets our core problem wrong. It's not sin. It was not that we were doing bad things – stealing, lying, cheating, committing sexual sins. It was not our bad behavior. Jesus did not die to just improve our behavior. We sin because of the death. Sin came from the death. Of course, in the garden, death came from the sin, but now sin comes from the death. We sinned because we were born spiritually dead to God. I don't mean that we have no spirit. We have a spirit. Our spirit is just dead to the things of God. When we are born again, our spirit is made alive to God and dead to sin. God works in our individual lives to bring us into intimate fellowship with Him, but when it comes to sin, it is not on an individual basis.

Through ONE MAN, sin entered the world and death through sin, and it spread to all men (Romans 5:12). WHY? Because according to Genesis 5:3, we were born as sons of Adam, born in his likeness, after his image. We were born "in Adam". We are his seed. But thank God, when we are born again, we are "In Christ" and no longer in Adam. We are now born of incorruptible seed (1Peter 1:23). The seed of Adam is not stronger than the seed of Jesus. The sin of Adam is not stronger than the righteousness of Christ! That's why 1 John 3:9 tells us, *"Whoever has been born of God **does not sin**, for His seed remains in him; and **he cannot sin**, because he has been born of God."* Most Christians do not understand what this verse means. Even though some translations say it means we don't "practice" sin, this is a mistranslation of the original Greek. The word "practice" does not appear in the original language. The verse means exactly what it says. *"Whoever has been born of God **does not sin**." WHY?* Because *"God's seed remains in him; and **he cannot sin**."*

One of the biggest problems that Christians have is understanding that we cannot sin and that we are completely righteous. This is because they do not understand the principle of spirit, soul, and body. I don't have the space in this chapter to deal with this, but let me say that the moment we are born again, our spirit is created just as righteous as Jesus (1 John 4:17), in true holiness, righteousness, glorious and has the very nature of Jesus Christ Himself (Ephesians 4:24). The Father made Jesus to be sin in our place so we could receive His Righteousness as a free gift (2 Corinthians 5:21).

When you primarily see sin as a noun instead of something you do, it will profoundly change your view of what Jesus did on the cross. You will see that grace is an active verb because grace is action. It is the action of Jesus on your behalf. You now see that Jesus Christ took SIN (the noun, the complete thing, the thing itself) unto Himself, rather than just taking one or two or many confessed sins (the verbs, the things we did). The difference is enormous. Meditate deeply on this revelation. Let it sink in and renew your mind. Jesus Christ has performed a complete work, a finished work, a fundamental change to this world. He took away the sin barrier between you and God. Grace is always an active verb because the Grace of God is always present and active to reach us and transform us.

Chapter 22

Myth: The New Testament Begins with Matthew, Chapter One

When did the New Testament begin? We must remember that the word "testament" means a person's will. Therefore, the New Covenant did not start with the birth of Jesus but with the death of Jesus. I understand that the New Testament is the name we give to the 27 books of the Bible, from Matthew through Revelation, but these books reveal and explain the New Testament. In the Bible, we find the words "heirs" and "inheritance" being used regarding believers.

> *and if children, then **heirs--heirs** of God and **joint heirs** with Christ, if indeed we suffer with Him, that we may also be glorified together.* (Romans 8:17)

> *giving thanks to the Father who has qualified us to be partakers of the **inheritance** of the saints in the light.* (Colossians 1:12)

For us, "heir" and "inherit" are words that have to do with a "will or testament." The Bible has two testaments, the Old and New Testament. The Old Covenant was an agreement between God and the children of Israel. The New Covenant is an agreement between God and Jesus Christ. Therefore, it includes all who are united with Jesus Christ, or as the Bible says, all those who are "in Christ." Both the Hebrew and Greek words used for "testament" in the Bible can also be translated to mean "covenant". Whenever the context had to do with relationship, it was translated as "covenant", and whenever the context was about inheritance, it was translated as "testament".

When Does a Testament Go into Effect?

A testament or will is enacted only after a person dies. An heir cannot inherit if the person who wrote the testament is still alive

> *[16] For where there is a testament, there must also of necessity be the death of the testator. [17] For a testament is in force after men are dead, since it has no power at all while the testator lives.* (Hebrews 9:16-17)

These verses in Hebrews make clear that the New Covenant could not begin until after the death of Jesus Christ. Why is it so important that we understand when the New Covenant actually began? Because it is the key to rightly dividing the Word of Truth (2 Timothy 2:15).

If you don't rightly divide the New Covenant from the Old Covenant, you will end up confused and double-minded. Many people do not clearly understand this, and so they incorrectly teach us about what our responsibilities are concerning the things Jesus taught (the words in red). Some say we must obey all the words in red (words that Jesus taught). Some say not all the words of Jesus were meant for us to obey. Which is it?

Before I answer, consider this: During the 30 years or so that Jesus lived on the earth and the three years that He ministered before He died, under which testament did He live? Remember that while Jesus was alive, the New Covenant had not yet begun. The Bible tells us that Jesus was born under the Law, to redeem those under the Law.

> *⁴ But when the fullness of the time had come, God sent forth His Son, born of a woman, born under the law, ⁵ to redeem those who were under the law, that we might receive the adoption as sons.* (Galatians 4:4-5)

We must remember that Jesus lived at the intersection of two different covenants. Jesus did not come to destroy the Old Covenant, but as our representative, He came to fulfill it (Matthew 5:17). Jesus kept the old Law, keeping covenant on our behalf so that we might relate to God through a new and better covenant. Since the New Covenant could not begin before He died, Jesus lived all His pre-cross life under the Old Covenant of the Law. Some people claim that we still must obey the Old Covenant Law simply because Jesus did. Jesus *had* to obey it because He was born under the Law to redeem those under the Law.

It is a mistake to directly apply every word Jesus said to our lives. We must consider to whom Jesus was speaking and His purpose. His audience was Jews who were under the Law. Jesus magnified the commands of the Law to expose the futility of trying to obtain righteousness by the Law. There are those today who teach that we must obey all the "words in red" that Jesus spoke in the New Testament. That's impossible. Jesus said things like *"if your right eye causes you to sin, pluck it out, and if your hand has caused you to sin, cut it off"* (Matthew 5:29-30).

Based on these "words in red," our churches should be filled with one-eyed amputees. Jesus said, *"Unless your righteousness exceeds the righteousness of the scribes and Pharisees, you will by no means enter the kingdom of heaven"* (Matthew 5:20). His Jewish listeners would have been shocked by this statement. The Scribes and Pharisees were the most righteous people they knew. How could they ever hope to exceed their righteousness? That's the point. Jesus was preaching hopelessness to all who would try to obtain righteousness by keeping the Law. Jesus said, *"Be perfect"* (Matthew 5:48). Anyone reading this think that you're perfect by your performance? I didn't think so. See how ridiculous it is to say that we must obey all the words Jesus said prior to the cross.

In His sermon on the mount in Matthew 5, Jesus said several times, *"You have heard it said, but I say unto you."* Jesus would then ramp up the meaning and true intent of the Law. For example, Jesus said, *"You have heard that it was said to those of old, 'You shall not commit adultery.' But I say to you that whoever looks at a woman to lust for her has already committed adultery with her in his heart"* (Matthew 5:27-28). That statement pretty much condemned every man as an adulterer according to the Law. Jesus did not want them to try harder to keep the Law. He wanted them to give up. Once they gave up, He could then show them the new and living way. He could show them that salvation is a gift by the Grace of God. He could reveal to them the new wine and the new wine skin.

If you compare the preaching of the Apostle Paul with the preaching of Jesus, their teachings are not the same. They seem to be at odds. Paul wrote epistles about life under the New Covenant. Jesus' teachings were aimed at the religious Jews and were meant to destroy their attempt to be made right with God by obeying the Law. After the cross, we see Paul and the other apostles preach a message of unconditional love, grace, and mercy to all who place their faith in Christ. The way that God relates to believers under the New Covenant is so vastly different from the way He related to Israel under the Law that it can't be even remotely compared.

The death of Jesus on the cross changed everything. Without a proper understanding of the context, some of the words of Jesus (before the cross) may seem contrary to what Paul the Apostle preached (after the cross). Jesus said the following:

And forgive us our debts, As we forgive our debtors. (Matthew 6:12)

But if you do not forgive, neither will your Father in heaven forgive your trespasses. (Mark 11:26)

Jesus' statements show us that, prior to the cross, our forgiveness from God was based on our ability to forgive others. That means that if we refuse to forgive others, God won't forgive us.

Paul, on the other hand, made the following statements:

And be kind to one another, tenderhearted, forgiving one another, just as God in Christ forgave you. (Ephesians 4:32)

bearing with one another, and forgiving one another, if anyone has a complaint against another; even as Christ forgave you, so you also must do. (Colossians 3:13)

Notice the forgiveness of God in the above verses is past tense. It is something God has done, not something that He will do if we forgive others. I also want to put out that the word "must" in Colossians 3:13 is italicized, which means it does not appear in the original language but was added by the translators. The Apostle John also echoes our forgiveness in 1 John 2:12, saying:

*I write to you, little children, because **your sins are forgiven you** for His name's sake.* Not will be, but have been forgiven.

Under the New Covenant, God considers those who believe in Him to be spotless and blameless in His sight. The book of Hebrews speaks about how this New Covenant would make us desire in our hearts what God desires and that we would no longer need the external rules of the Law to say no to sin. We would want to say no to sin from our hearts.

[16] *"This is the covenant that I will make with them after those days, says the LORD: I will put My laws into their hearts, and in their minds I will write them,"* [17] *then He adds, "Their sins and their lawless deeds I will remember no more."* (Hebrews 10:16-17)

Under this New Covenant, we don't have to forgive others in order to receive our own forgiveness. I am not saying that unforgiveness is okay and that it doesn't matter if you forgive people or not. I'm saying we *need* to forgive. Forgiveness is for our own good.

Without a clear understanding of when the New Covenant starts and what the New Covenant is, we will be confused. Every word spoken by Jesus before His resurrection was spoken before the New Covenant existed. Does this mean we should ignore what Jesus said before His resurrection, or that what He said was not true? Of course not! Jesus is the Truth! It just means we need to remember He was talking to people under the Old Covenant, not the New Covenant. Under the Old Covenant, keeping the commandments was required as the way to have good standing with God. Under the New Covenant, good standing with God is a gift that comes with believing in Jesus Christ. The entire New Testament is Jesus' message to us, not just the words in red. What most of the church doesn't realize is that when people were first introduced to the red-letter Bible (the words of Jesus printed in red), they bought them up immediately, thinking that this was truly the work of the Holy Spirit. Yet they never knew that it was not so much about the words of Jesus in red as it was a marketing gimmick to sell Bibles that were different from mainstream Bibles at the time. Yet Americans were quick to latch onto it, thus creating a traditional mindset of "Red letter only" scripture. The words in black are just as inspired by the Holy Spirit as the words in red. The things He said to His body – the church – after He redeemed us with His Blood take precedence over the words He spoke under His Old Covenant ministry on earth. So, don't be confused and think what Jesus said during earthly ministry was His complete, total, and final word. In fact, Jesus said:

¹² I still have many things to say to you, but you cannot bear them now. ¹³ However, when He, the Spirit of truth, has come, He will guide you into all truth; for He will not speak on His own authority, but whatever He hears He will speak; and He will tell you things to come. (John 16:12-13)

If Jesus had already given them all the truth, there wouldn't have been a need for the Holy Spirit to come and guide them into all truth. Jesus continued speaking through His apostles after His ascension to heaven. This is what we have recorded as the letters to the church (Romans through Revelation) in the New Testament. Through these letters, Jesus by the Holy Spirit has revealed that the New Covenant includes right standing with God as a free gift through our union with Jesus Christ our Lord!

Chapter 23

Myth: The Greatest Need of the Church Today Is Revival

The word "revival" is never once mentioned in the New Testament – not once. Nor do we see the early church seeking revival. None of the New Testament apostles prayed for or ever mentioned "revival" or "revive us". This should at least make us all give pause and think about why we keep uttering this phrase when it was never found in the New Testament! I understand there are other words that are not specifically mentioned in the Bible that we believe in. For example, the word "Bible" is not in the Bible. The word "Trinity" is not in the Bible. Yet we know and believe in the Bible and the Trinity. However, this is not true with "revival". Revival has become such a common theme in churches that it seems almost blasphemous to suggest that revival is not the churches' greatest need today.

The church I grew up in was one where revival was preached, prayed, and prophesied about continually. We all have heard it: "Lord, send revival to our church." "Please, God, send revival to our land." "Lord, we need a revival." Revival is the cry of the church, or is it? The main problem I have with crying for God to send revival is that it implies that the problem is on God's end, that somehow, we need to convince God to do something, that He's holding back from us something we need. God loves the people you're praying for much more than you do.

We pray for things that we already possess. This is a major problem in the church today. We don't know what we've been given through the finished work of Jesus. We pray for the "mind of Christ," when the Bible says we already have the mind of Christ (1 Corinthians 2:16). We pray for God to pour out His Spirit, when He already has on all flesh (Acts 2:16-17). We pray for an open Heaven, yet the heavens were opened at Jesus' baptism (Matthew 3:16). The only place the heavens are closed is between our ears. We pray that God would go with us as we leave the church building, when God promised that He would never leave us, nor forsake us.

The reason many within the church today are constantly seeking another revival is simply because they do not understand what they already have right now. They are ignorant of the power and authority they have already been given because of the cross, plus the arrival of the Holy Spirit who indwells believers. When Christ went to the cross, He fulfilled everything that needed to be filled on the cross. Now we have the *"fullness of Him"* (Ephesians 1:23). We are *"complete in Him"* (Colossians 2:9-10). We have already been (not "going to be," but "have been") *"blessed with every spiritual blessing in the heavenly places in Christ"* (Ephesians 1:3).

So, if revival is not the greatest need of the church today, what is? We need revelation of what God has already done. The Apostle Paul never prayed for revival, but he did pray that "the spirit of wisdom and revelation in the knowledge of Him" be given to us.

> *[16] do not cease to give thanks for you, making mention of you in my prayers: [17] that the God of our Lord Jesus Christ, the Father of glory, may give to you the spirit of wisdom and revelation in the knowledge of Him, [18] the eyes of your understanding being enlightened; that you may know what is the hope of His calling, what are the riches of the glory of His inheritance in the saints ,[19] and what is the exceeding greatness of His power toward us who believe, according to the working of His mighty power* (Ephesians 1:16-19)

Notice that Paul was not asking God to send revival, but that the revelation of what God has already done would be known by the believers. He prayed that our eyes would be enlightened; that you would have a full revelation of your potential in Christ Jesus, that you could see what the riches of the glory of your inheritance are as a saint.

There's a big difference between revival and revelation of the finished work of Jesus. "Revival" says, "Give me a spiritual B-12 shot. Get me fired up about Jesus again." The word "revive" means to "bring back to life." When you were born again, you were given eternal life, not temporary life. You were not given your old life with a new paint job. You were given a whole new life because you are a whole new creation in Christ. When you begin to see what Jesus really accomplished for you and me on the cross, it will radically change all your past assumptions concerning our need to be revived.

Although the Bible uses the word "revive" in the Old Testament, this term must be understood in the context of Israel's apostasy and their constant need to be called back to a relationship with God. Revival, therefore, had an entirely different connotation then. Revival today means so many different things to different people. To some, it means a few nightly church services with a guest preacher. To others, it means a sovereign move of the Holy Spirit like The Great Awakening in the eighteenth century.

In the revival movement of today, the common practice has been for churches to call in a revival preacher to instill new life into the congregation, to encourage people to make a "decision for Christ," and for their members of the church to "rededicate their lives to the Lord." Besides the fact that this decisional and rededication type of preaching is unbiblical, my biggest problem is that it teaches people to expect what God has done in their lives to fade away.

That's the reason churches usually schedule a spring and a fall revival, and don't be surprised to see the same people who "rededicated" their lives last revival doing it all again in the next revival. In our church growing up, it was not uncommon for revivals to run for several weeks straight, and at the conclusion of the revival, the number of salvations would be reported. I would hear that forty people were saved, and yet a week after the revival ended, we couldn't find any of those forty who were saved. I'm not saying the numbers were fabricated or exaggerated, but something was wrong in our approach. It was more emotional than experiential. We needed to do more than get excited about Jesus. We needed a change in thinking and in our understanding of forgiveness and grace. We needed a revelation in the knowledge of Him.

The truth is, and let's be clear about this, revivals never last. They were never meant to. The main reason revivals don't last is because of the way we approach revival. They get excited, they run, they shout, they have an *emotional experience* that is very powerful and they are convinced this is the "Holy Spirit moving" and they ride that wave of high emotions and excitement, but within weeks, they have a spiritual crash. The high of the "revival" is gone, so what do they say? You guessed it. They say, "We need *another* revival!"

I remember hearing a Methodist pastor's comments to a Charismatic pastor. He stated, "I know what's wrong with you Charismatics and Pentecostals. You try to live in a constant state of revival." I think there is some truth to his statement. I see people that strain to be what they perceive to be a "revived" person. They will burn out quickly. It's like driving a car at top speed all the time. Eventually, something is going to break. And yet once again, good Christians fall into a religious routine. They have to have another revival, and once *that* revival is over, they go back to their lives and their day jobs, hoping that the fresh fire they experienced will last. But for most, it doesn't, and they become disillusioned. Some end up drying up spiritually, and some even leave the church, much worse for the wear.

I am not in any way disparaging people who call on God for hope and for a fresh renewal. I am not discounting the genuine move of God. What I am against is our making people believe that what they have been given when they were born again has faded away, that they need an event to get them pumped up. That is why we need our eyes opened to the gift of the Holy Spirit active in our lives, that the same Spirit that raised Jesus from the dead DWELLS (not visits) in us, and He will give life to our mortal bodies (Romans 8:11). We need to walk in this revelation in our personal lives, rather than waiting on the "next" move.

If the greatest need of the church today is for revival, then what's the purpose of the gospel? After all, it is the foolishness of preaching which saves them who believe (1 Corinthians 1:21), not revival. The truth is God has already done everything that the Church needs in these last days – everything. There is nothing we need to add to the work of the cross, or the Holy Spirit, other than keeping our eyes fixed on Jesus, the author and finisher of our faith, and allowing the Holy Spirit to work this revelation into our daily lives. You and I are renewed daily, because we believe in what Jesus did on the cross. We've been given something greater than a revival, something much deeper and more substantial, and it is centered on our knowing the grace and the goodness of our God. Any thoughts or beliefs that make us think God is distant and unapproachable or that God is anything less than love must be challenged and changed at the core. We don't need revival, we need something better. We need the revelation of the finished work of Jesus Christ on the cross!

Chapter 24

Myth: Satan Needs God's Permission to Attack a Believer

Does Satan Need God's Permission to Attack a Believer?

[31] And the Lord said, "Simon, Simon! Indeed, satan has asked for you, that he may sift you as wheat. [32] But I have prayed for you, that your faith should not fail; and when you have returned to Me, strengthen your brethren." (Luke 22:31-32)

There are those who teach and believe that satan needs God's permission to attack us. They believe that God gives satan permission to attack us. Would you give a vicious enemy, one whose desire is to kill, steal, and destroy, permission to attack your child? No? I didn't think so. Why would you believe that God would do that to you? Is that what's going on in the verses above? Is Jesus giving satan permission to "sift" Peter? I don't think so. First of all, satan in the Bible is called "the thief." He comes to kill, steal, and destroy. If a thief has "permission" to steal, then he can't be called a thief.

The Message translation says it well. *"Simon, stay on your toes. Satan has tried his best to separate all of you from me, like chaff from wheat"* (Luke 22:31).

The word "sift" means to separate. Jesus is telling Peter that satan wants to separate him from Jesus. The word "you" is plural. Jesus is letting Peter know that satan's plan is to try and separate all of the disciples from Him.

The KJV says, "Satan hath desired to have you." The Greek word translated here "desired" means "to demand for trial." How could satan demand Peter for trial? We must remember that this is prior to Jesus going to the cross. And we must also remember that God had given the earth to Adam, but Adam gave it to satan in the garden.

[16] The heaven, even the heavens, are the LORD'S; But the earth He has given to the children of men. (Psalm 115:16)

In the temptation of Jesus in the wilderness, satan says to Jesus: *"All this authority I will give You, and their glory; for this has been delivered to me, and I give it to whomever I wish"* (Luke 4:6). When did this "delivery" take place? When Adam handed control and authority of the planet over to satan in the garden.

For those who insist that God gives satan permission to attack His children, they point to the one of the oldest and most misunderstood books in the Bible – the story of Job. Trying to read the Bible without a deep appreciation for the Grace of God and the finished work of Jesus Christ on the cross will leave you confused. To understand the written word, you must know the Living Word.

As I'm sure you know, Job was a man who lost everything. Most Christians believe that God set Job up for attack by dangling him in front of satan like a pork chop to a hungry bulldog. This portrays God and satan working in partnership. The devil attacked Job, but God permitted it. He "allowed" it to happen. This whole "God allowed it" doctrine that has invaded the church has impugned the name of God. I've heard statements like, "I got cancer, but God allowed it to happen for His purposes. He's trying to teach me something."

How ridiculous! Statements like this are not only ignorant, but also blasphemous. God does not inflict cancer and sickness on us to teach us stuff. God is more than capable of disciplining (i.e., training) us through His Word (2 Timothy 3:16).

The sad thing with this lie is that the underlying premise is that if you've been attacked by satan, then God "allowed it." There isn't much you can do about is because that would go against God's will. That if you're suffering, you must have done something bad. God must be punishing you. This is one of the oldest lies in history and can be traced back to our misunderstanding of the book of Job. I can understand how at first glance it seems that God is giving the devil permission to go after Job. But, when you read the account of Job in a literal translation such as Young's Literal Translation, you will get a more accurate meaning of the original Hebrew language:

And Jehovah saith unto the Adversary, "Hast thou set thy heart against My servant Job because there is none like him in the land, a man perfect and upright, fearing God, and turning aside from evil?" (Job 1:8, YLT)

Look at Green's Literal Translation of the Holy Bible (LITV):

And Jehovah said to satan, Have you set your heart on My servant Job because there is none like him in the earth, a perfect and upright man, fearing God and turning away from evil? (Job 1:8, LITV)

Satan had set his heart to attack Job. God was letting satan know that He knew what he was up to. Well, why didn't God just stop the devil? He couldn't. I didn't say He didn't have the power to stop him, but God really gave the earth to man, and now because of man giving that power to satan, he had authority to attack man. God does not control everything that happens on this earth. Much of what happens is not His Will. In fact, the Bible never says God is in control, but it does say that the devil has control:

We know that we are children of God, and that the whole world is under the control of the evil one. (1 John 5:19 NIV).

When God said to satan, *"All that he has is in thy power"* (Job 1:12, see also 2:6), He wasn't handing Job over to the devil. God doesn't make deals with the devil. He was simply stating a fact. That because of the fall, satan had authority on the earth and over men. Job was already under the dominion of satan. This was demonstrated again when satan contended with Michael the archangel over the body of Moses (Jude 1:9). Satan felt like he owned all men, even Moses.

Here are some things we need to keep in mind. We are disciples of Jesus, not disciples of Job. Job was the question. Jesus is the answer.

Job wasn't saved. He wasn't filled with the Holy Spirit. Job had some understanding of God, but not every statement that Job said about God was correct. Like many Christians today, Job thought that God was the cause of all his suffering and loss. That's why he said, "The Lord gave, and the Lord has taken away." Really? Does God give and then take away what He gave? That sounds more like a thief. Does God give parents a child, and then just decide to take it away? No wonder so many people hate God because this verse was quoted at their child's funeral. God would never do that. He said His gifts are *irrevocable*, never rescinded (Romans 11:29). *"Children are a gift from the Lord; they are a reward from him"* (Psalm 127:3 NLT).

Job admitted that he spoke things that he did not understand and which he did not know (Job 42:3). Job said that he had only heard of God, but when his eyes saw Him, Job said, "I hate myself." Job hated that he had a wrong opinion of God. The book of Job is an inferior revelation of God. I didn't say an inaccurate revelation, just one that wasn't not complete. Jesus Christ is a superior revelation of God, and I will not form my total view of God from Job.

Like Job, many today have a wrong opinion of who God is, of His nature, character, and attributes. To get a view of God and His character, one only needs to look at Jesus, not Job. When you have seen Jesus, you have seen God the Father (John 14:9). Jesus is the express image of His Father (Hebrews 1:3). We need to question anything we think we know about God that we cannot see in the life of Jesus. Can you really picture Jesus killing people, stealing their belongings, or allowing satan to attack them? Of course not. So why would you think that God would do those things?

Some Final Thoughts

The Bible tells us that the Son of God was manifested to destroy the works of the devil (1John 3:8), not to work as partner with him. It also tells us that God disarmed principalities and powers on the cross (Colossians 2:15), but that begs the question of why God would rearm the devil who He had just disarmed? Paul the Apostle says that when we are saved, we are "in Christ," that we are the temple of God (2 Corinthians 5:17; 1 Corinthians 3:16). Why would God give the devil permission to attack His temple? So, if I am in Him, and He is in me then it would be tantamount to the devil asking God for permission to attack Jesus. How ludicrous is that?

Satan is always whispering in the ear of those who are suffering, "Don't go running to God about your pain or trouble. He gave me permission to attack you! Just look at Job!"

Job is only mentioned one time in the New Testament. Here is the Message translation of that verse:

> *What a gift life is to those who stay the course! You've heard, of course, of Job's staying power, and you know how God brought it all together for him at the end. That's because God cares, cares right down to the last detail* (James 5:11 *MSG*).

From the beginning to the end, it is always satan's purpose to harm us. It is always God's will to bless us. This simple theology will greatly help you – God good, devil bad.

Chapter 25

The Myth of More

If you were satan and you wanted to tempt Adam and Eve into sinning against God, how would you do it? What lie would you use? How can you tempt them when they have need of nothing? They lack nothing. They have been provided everything they will ever need. Yet, satan convinced them that they needed more and that God had not provided everything they needed. This lie served satan well in the garden and is one that he has been using successfully on the church ever since.

The church culture that I grew up around was one of constantly crying out for more. We would pray for more of God, for more faith, for more anointing, for more, more, more. I would often hear the phrase "more of Him and less of me." Prayers like "Lord may I decrease, so that you can increase" were a common request. You may be thinking, "What's wrong with the cry for more?" Because it insinuates that the problem is on God's end, that He has withheld things that we need from us, and that all our problems could be solved if He would just grant us more of Him. God can't give you any more of Himself than He has already given you. You have been given Christ Jesus. The fullness of the Godhead dwells within you by His Spirit.

> *⁹ For in Him dwells all the fullness of the Godhead bodily; ¹⁰ and* **you are complete in Him,** *who is the head of all principality and power.* (Colossians 2:9-10)

You have been given His "fullness," not His "half-ness"! You are complete in Him! *"And of His fullness we have all received, and grace for grace"* (John 1:16). God – by grace – has already provided everything we'll ever need. It's not a matter of asking God to provide more, but rather us believing in what we've been given, and releasing and manifesting what we already possess.

Let me say that the sincere desire to see more faith, anointing, and healings manifested is wonderful. What's not wonderful is the wrong belief that our problem is lack, that God has not already given us everything we need. The Bible teaches that God **has given** (not will give) us ALL THINGS that pertain to life and godliness.

> *² Grace and peace be multiplied to you in the knowledge of God and of Jesus our Lord, ³ as His divine power* **has given to us all things** *that pertain to life and godliness, through the knowledge of Him who called us by glory and virtue,* (2 Peter 1:2-3)

> *³ Blessed be the God and Father of our Lord Jesus Christ,* **who has blessed us with every spiritual blessing** *in the heavenly places in Christ,* (Ephesians 1:3)

I realize this is hard for some to believe, but the only thing that we are lacking is knowledge. You will not find any of the apostles praying for more of God in the New Testament. The Apostle Paul never prayed for "more of God," but he did pray that "the spirit of wisdom and revelation in the knowledge of Him" be given to us. We waste time and energy praying for things that we already possess. This is a major problem in the church today. We don't know what we've been given through the finished work of Jesus. We pray for the "mind of Christ," when the Bible clearly says we already have the mind of Christ (1 Corinthians 2:16). We pray for God to pour out His Spirit. He already has on all flesh (Acts 2:16-17). We pray for an open Heaven; the heavens were opened at Jesus' baptism (Matthew 3:16). The only place the heavens are closed is between our ears. We pray that God would go with us as we leave the church building, when God promised that He would never leave us, nor forsake us.

When I was young in the ministry, we would have "double portion prayer lines." We would tell people that if they wanted a "double portion" of God's spirit to come forward for prayer, and we would lay our hands on them to receive this double portion. We were sincere, but sincerely wrong! Guess where we took our scripture reference for this from the Bible? The Old Covenant. You can't preach or find "double portion" theology from the New Testament. It's not there. You cannot receive double. You already have His fullness. You are not lacking anything You are complete in Him. Over the years, I've had people ask me to pray for them because they didn't feel God's love. They wanted me to pray that God would pour His Love into them. I can't pray for that. Why? Because it would be calling God a liar to pray for what He has already done. Romans 5:5 says, "*The love of God **has been poured out in our hearts** by the Holy Spirit who was given to us.*" Not that His Love *will be* poured out if we pray.

If you're not experiencing God's love for you, it's not that God hasn't given it. His Love has been poured out into your heart whether you feel it or not! It's important for you to understand that His Love has been poured in your heart—in other words, in your spirit. He *"has blessed us with all spiritual blessings in heavenly places in Christ."* It says those spiritual blessings are in heavenly places in Christ, but they are in you because *you* are in Christ. Some may say, "Well, it says that they're spiritual blessings." That's correct. It's all in the realm of the spirit.

You are a spirit and a soul that has a body. It's essential for you to understand this. When you were "born again," your spirit man was born again. In your born-again spirit, you are just like Jesus (1John 4:17). You are one spirit with Him, joined in spirit to Him (1Corinthians. 6:17). Your new spirit was created in righteousness and true holiness (Ephesians 4:24). It was created that way. It is not a process of becoming that way. It was made righteous and holy when you were born again. The new you is truly new, yet you still have an old mind and body. Our mind (soul) and body needs renewing (Romans 12: 1-2). The key to victorious living as a believer is learning to live out of your new born-again spirit instead of the old man.

God has already provided everything for us in the spirit realm. I can hear some asking, "If this is true, how do we manifest in the natural realm what He has provided in the spiritual realm?" First, stop praying for what you already have. We need to "repent". The word "repent" means to think differently. We need to think and speak differently than we have in the past. So, instead of praying prayers like, "Lord, I ask you to be with me this week, to bless me," say, "Father, I thank you that you'll never leave me, that you're always with me and for me, that you have blessed me with everything I will ever need through Christ Jesus." When you have faith in God and His Word, it takes the struggle out of faith. Since God has already provided it, faith is simple. It's not a struggle. Faith is not us trying to get God to provide something. It's simply our receptive response to what He's already provided.

I know that many will struggle with these truths because they are so contrary to what they are presently experiencing in the natural. I'm not asking you to deny the natural realm or to deny the physical things that you're presently experiencing. I'm just asking you to deny that the natural realm is all that there is. You must believe far more than just what your five senses reveal. God is Spirit (John 4:24). He moves in the spirit realm. Faith *"calls those things which do not exist as though they did"* (Romans 4:17). Faith believes in God's goodness, agrees with God, and calls things that are already done in the spirit to be manifested into the natural realm.

Seeing Is Not Believing

This is a popular saying in the world: "Seeing is believing." But this is contrary to the word of God. Jesus told Martha in John 11: 40, *"Did I not say to you that if you would believe you would see the glory of God?"* The believing comes before the seeing. This should not be so foreign to us because we believe in many things we cannot see. We believe that there are television and radio signals in the atmosphere, even though we can't see them. We can see those signals that are invisible to our senses manifested just by turning on our television or radio. We need to begin to apply this to our spiritual thinking. Just like those signals that are there and have been provided for us, we need to receive them. We need to allow our faith to be the receiver for what grace has freely provided.

I want to make a statement that may seem controversial at first, but allow me to explain. God is not going to forgive anyone today of their sin no matter how much they beg Him to do so. The truth is that He has already forgiven the world of sin. When Jesus died on the cross, He said, *"It is finished"* (John 19:30). Jesus is now seated at the right hand of the Father. He is seated because His Work is finished. Do you need forgiveness? Then just receive it. Forgiveness is not something that God does. It's something He's done. I've explained this in detail in several chapters in this book. It's not a matter of *if* God will forgive you. He's *already* forgiven the sins of the whole world (1 John 2:2). Will you receive His Forgiveness? Will you put faith in the finished work of Jesus? That's the real issue.

Let me explain this another way. God is not going to decide to "save" someone today. Often over the years, women have come up to me and asked me to pray that God would "save their lost husband." They would tell me that they have prayed for him to be saved for years, and "God has not saved him yet." The problem is not God's giving of grace. It is the husband's receiving of that grace and salvation. Do you see the difference? It is huge! God desires her husband to be saved more than she does. He's not withholding His Salvation from him. I will not pray and ask God to save her husband as if the problem is on God's end, but I will pray and ask God that this man will hear the good news of the Gospel and believe and be saved.

While many will accept the truth that the forgiveness of sin was accomplished 2,000 years ago when Jesus shed His Blood and many will put their faith in that sacrifice today and be saved, many will struggle when this is applied to their healing. Many cry out to God for Him to come down and heal them today of their sickness, yet the Bible says, "By His stripes you WERE healed" (1Peter 2:24). Not will be healed, but WERE healed. When were you and I forgiven of sin? Two-thousand years ago when Jesus shed His Blood. When did we receive and enjoy the benefit of that forgiveness? When we believed. That may have been ten years ago, but the point is that God was not withholding your forgiveness. God did not just decide to save you the day you were born again. That was just the day that you believed in Him and received His Salvation.

He would have saved you years before if you had only believed. In like manner, when were you and I healed? The answer is the same – 2000 years ago when Jesus was striped for our healing! The question is not "Will God heal us?" The question is "Will we believe that the price has already been paid for our healing and will we receive that healing by faith in Him?" The problem is that many Christians are "looking forward to their healing" instead of "looking back to when they were healed." They look forward to healing as a possible future event that God will either decide to do for them or not.

Let me ask you this: Do you believe that God just decides to save some people and decides not to save others? Is that the God you believe in? The Bible says that it's not His Will that ANY should perish, but that all come to repentance (2 Peter 3:9). If you believe that anyone can receive salvation by putting their faith in the finished work of Jesus, then you also must believe that anyone can receive their healing by placing their faith in the finished work of Jesus. Jesus paid the price for both, our forgiveness, and our healing. The problem occurs when we fail to manifest our healing. When there is a delay in us experiencing healing in our bodies, this leads to some of the flaky beliefs in the church.

Some have been told that the reason their healing has not manifested is that God has allowed their sickness, that He is teaching them something. What a lie! For some strange reason, people seem to find comfort in believing that God is responsible for their sickness. I've noticed that even Christians who believe the lie that God is responsible for their sickness and that He's "allowed" it for some divine purpose will rush to their medical doctors to get healed of their sickness or disease. If they really believed that God is behind their sickness, then why try to get rid of it? Just stay sick and learn as much as you can. Do you not see how foolish this belief it? The Lord would no more put sickness on a New Testament believer than He would cause us to sin. God is not the author of my sickness or pain. He is the author and finisher of our faith (Hebrews 12:2). This has changed my view of Him more than anything else has.

My theology has become rather simple: God good, devil bad. If it is good, it is from God. If it's bad, it's not from my Father. Maybe you came to God because of something bad or painful in your life that overwhelmed you and caused you to turn to Him for help. That pain or circumstance, even though because of it you came to the Lord, was not from Him, regardless of the outcome. It was your faith that you placed in His Grace that turned your life around, not the problem.

Chapter 26

A Final Word

I wrote this book with the hope that it would help those who read it to never live one moment without the revelation of God's Amazing Grace. Most of my Christian life was one of hoping that I would make it to Heaven when I died, although I never felt assured that I would. My relationship with God was one of always trying to please Him, trying to keep, and obey the Law and the religious rules of my denomination. I felt God was angry with me at times. I never felt like I had prayed enough, read enough, or fasted enough. My praying and Bible reading was a way of making God like me more, to please Him more, a way to make myself a fit vessel that He would anoint and use.

In more than three decades of going to church, I never heard one message about the Grace of God. When I did hear grace mentioned, it was always in the negative. Terms like greasy grace, cheap grace. I knew that I was saved by grace through faith, but then I was told that my salvation, forgiveness, and acceptance by

God were now maintained by my keeping the rules. Grace was more of a theological term than an actual experience. We would sing the song, "Amazing Grace," but few seemed really amazed by His Grace.

There is much confusion in the church today about grace. Some think grace is their "get out of jail free card." They don't know what grace is. They have a concept, but they don't have grace. Grace isn't a bunch of rules for you to keep. Grace is a Person living His Life through you. Grace has eyes. Noah found grace in the eyes of the Lord (Genesis 6:8). Many in the church today have missed the Grace of God because they're not looking in His eyes. Grace is not a theology. It is not another subject in the Bible. Grace is the subject of the Bible. It is not a doctrine. It is a Person, and His name is Jesus. That's the reason the Lord wants you to receive the abundance of grace, for to have the abundance of grace is to have the abundance of Jesus.

The Law was given, but grace and truth came (John 1:17). Jesus didn't come to teach grace, but to be grace. People who don't understand what or who Grace is either misuse it or they attack it. Grace stopped me from always taking my own temperature, trying to see if I was right with God. Now I know I'm right with God through Jesus Christ. When you have looked into the eyes of grace, it will not lead you into sin. I've been married over thirty-seven years. Never once has my wife's love for me made me think, "You know, she loves me so much, I can now sleep with anyone I want and she will still love me."

Grace is the revelation of absolute acceptance by God. It was the revelation that I'm completely forgiven, that I'm righteous now and always based on the finished work of Jesus on the cross. Grace doesn't mean that we're free **to**, but grace means we're free **from**. Free from what? I'm free from the Law, free from performance, free from my own self effort and labor. I can now relax and rest in the finished work of Jesus.

Since I've been preaching the revelation of grace, I've seen my church come alive to the goodness of God and what Jesus accomplished on the cross. The revelation of grace affects our view of God and our love for Jesus. Grace is the one thing that sets Christianity apart from all other religions in the world. It is not turning from sin, prayer, confession, or moral living. It is grace. Grace is unique only to us. This is a move of the Holy Spirit. It is an awakening to the Grace of God. It's going on inside every denomination and most churches. Christians all over the world are tasting the goodness of God's grace that leads us to repent (think differently), and they will never again settle for the mixture of Law and grace.

If this book has been a blessing and an encouragement in your walk with the Lord, I'd like to invite you to visit my website at *www.dellyoung.net*. There you will find more resources to help you in your own grace walk.

Dell Young
Points of Grace
4169 Quail Run Circle
Valdosta, GA 31601
229-561-1419
dellyoung8@gmail.com

Acknowledgments

I first want to acknowledge Jesus Christ, my Lord, and my God. Thank you for Your amazing grace and Your endless goodness that has revealed to us Your true nature.

To Jill, my beautiful wife, my most faithful supporter, encourager, and co-laborer in the ministry. I could not have made it this far without you by my side. You are God's gift to me, to our children, our grandchildren, and our church family. I love you with all my heart.

To Justin, my oldest son, thank you for your love, support, and encouragement. Thanks, son, for the years that you have served alongside me in ministry. You are an awesome drummer, musician, speaker, and entrepreneur. You started playing drums in church at five years of age. Thanks for still doing that every Sunday. Thanks for helping me minister the gospel on radio, internet, and television. You helped me believe far much more than I ever would have on my own. Thank you for connecting me with Michelle Prince and Prince Performance Group who published this book. They are amazing!

To my daughter Kristin, you are such a special delight and treasure of my life. You will always be "daddy's girl." Thank you for always doing your best to protect me and defend me from the attacks of religious people. Thank you not only your encouragement, but also your participation in my ministry. Thank you for loving God.

To Austin, my youngest son, thank you, son, for all your love, respect, and support that you've given me all these years. Thank you for mowing church grounds, working under your big brother's authority, and helping in the ministry. I love you, son. I have watched you handle health challenges with such courage. You have encouraged me so many times in the way you have kept going, accomplishing so much in your life. I'm proud to be your dad.

To John Tanner, my son in the Lord, the husband of my daughter, thank you for your love and encouragement. Thank you for helping me when I transitioned my ministry to GracePoint. You are a great worship leader, songwriter, musician, and business owner. I love you, John, very much.

To my two daughters-in-law, Brandi and Lora Young, thank you for loving my sons and blessing me with grandchildren. Thank you for the love, respect, and support you have given me in ministry. I love you both.

To my dad and mom (Paul and Ann Young), thank you both for all your love, support, and encouragement to me in my life and the ministry. Thank you for being there physically in the church, and showing your love and support. I love you both so much.

To the staff and the Elders of GracePoint Church, thank you for believing in me and the message of grace that God has given me. Thank you, Elder Crawford Powell, for bringing this project before the Elders. Thank you, Elders, for not only your support and encouragement in the publishing of this book, but your unwavering faithfulness, encouragement, and support to me from the first day we met. Thank you, Ron Butler. You are such an encourager to me and His body. Your boldness and dedication to make a difference speak volumes of your heart for God. To Ivory Lucas, such a man of honor and commitment for God and his family. To Crawford Powell, thanks for your encouragement, prophetic insight, and friendship. To Andy Fletcher, your servant's heart is without equal. Thanks for your genuine care and love. To Ken Marshall, thanks for your continued support and encouragement. You are a powerful example of integrity. To Billy Ray Lee, you are an Elder, Staff Pastor, friend, and the most faithful man that I've ever met. Thank you for all the many years of love and support that you've given me.

To Johanna Vrboncic, my church administrator, thanks for your faithfulness, love, and support. You are an amazing woman of God. Great is your reward! To David Hewitt, our Children's Pastor, and his wife Teresa and their entire team. Thank you for teaching God's kids how valuable they are to Him and how much He loves them. To Pastor Adam Page and his wife Lisa, Wow, you guys rock! Thanks for leading our student ministry, Bridge, with such passion. Your passion has ignited far greater fires than you can imagine. I am looking forward to sharing this adventure of ministry with you. Love you lots! To Ben and Liz James, my spiritual son and daughter, thank you for your love, support, and encouragement. Words simply cannot describe the love and affection that Jill and I feel toward you both. You have proven your hearts to us. You have looked upon Haiti and have been moved with compassion to save the lives of the children. We love what you're doing for God's kids.

To all my staff and Elders, it is a pleasure to work with each of you and an honor to serve God together. Jill and I love each of you very much.

To Pastor Martin Collins, thank you for your love and support to me for many years as an Elder, Staff Pastor, and friend. Having you by my side through those early days of ministry here was such a strength and blessing. You have your own ministry now. Please know that you remain deeply loved and missed over here. Bless you for your gentle spirit that ministers love and your compassion to all who meet you.

To Apostle L.A. Joiner, my spiritual father, thank you for all that you have poured into my life and ministry since I connected with you in 1997. I love you very much and thank you for your help, honesty, and encouragement. Thank you for letting me be me. Thank you for always being there when I needed you. I have learned much from you about the apostolic and spiritual fathering over these many years. It was a pleasure to serve on your apostolic team and to still be your adopted spiritual son today.

To Pastor Keith Stith, my spiritual son, thank you for your encouragement, trust, support, and your unfailing love toward me. You are a MASSIVE inspiration to me. Your faith in God and His Word has impacted me in so many ways - thank you. I have never met a man that has gone through so much physical adversity and yet remains so full of hope, faith, and trust in God. Thank you for your leadership at the House of Grace Ministry in Sparks,

Georgia. You are pouring God's grace into men who have never seen it before. Your life and ministry have touched countless lives.

To my Apostolic Team, Dr. Bennie Calloway, your life, your ministry, and your writings and wisdom have impacted so many people in so many ways. Thank you – you are a true gem. I admire and love you. To Pastor John Lewis, thank you for your love and support. Thank you for jumping into this grace river with me. Thanks for your courageous leadership and your stand for truth. Your dedication, sincerity, and love inspire all who know you. To Pastor Maxie Williams, thank you for your boldness to step out in faith and be part of this GracePoint family and Kingdom-Change Ministries, and to refuse to serve religious traditions. You're an inspiration to so many. To Pastors Martin Collins, Keith Stith, and Billy Ray Lee, thanks for helping me pastor and mentor leaders. I couldn't do it without you.

To Dr. Ron Cottle, a spiritual father, patriarch, and general to me and so many others in the body of Christ. Thank you for being such a great example to me. Thank you for the admonition, encouragement, and love that you have shown to me. Thank you for still running this race with us and motivating us to stay the course.

To all my sons and daughters in our Kingdom-Change Ministries, GracePoint Church family, and our ministerial friends all over the world, thank you for the deposit you have made in my life and ministry. Please forgive me for not being able to list all your names here. Space doesn't permit me to do so.

And lastly, to all the Grace Preachers that have had to defend their preaching, teaching, and writing as the Apostle Paul did in the New Covenant, I bless you. Thank you for carrying the message of

God's Grace to the world. I want to name a few that have greatly influenced my life, my preaching, and my writing: Joseph Prince, Andrew Wommack, Andrew Farley, Dr. Steve McVey, and Paul Ellis. You are a great blessing and inspiration to me. I'm so thankful to the Holy Spirit for leading me into the revelation of His Amazing Grace. Father God, thank you for all you have done for me and Your people through the finished work of Jesus on the cross. I don't have the words to adequately express what Your grace means to me.

And of His fullness we have all received, and grace for grace. (John 1:16)

About the Author

Dell Young serves as the Senior Pastor of GracePoint Church in Valdosta, Georgia. He is the founder of Kingdom-Change Ministries, which was established to help mentor and encourage ministry and marketplace leaders. He is also the founder of Cornerstone Church in Sparks, Georgia, and the founder of what is now Cook Christian Academy in Adel, Georgia. He has helped start, strengthen, and support churches for over twenty years. He has many spiritual sons and daughters that look to him for personal encouragement, insight, and wisdom.

Pastor Dell ministers with an emphasis on the Grace of God, realizing that grace is the loving kindness of our Father, poured out on us through Jesus Christ. He has been preaching and pastoring for more than thirty-one years. He holds a bachelor's degree in Theology from Christian Life School of Theology in Columbus, Georgia. He worked for twenty years as a paramedic and was the Chief of Tift County Emergency Medical Service for twelve years.

He is eminently qualified as a leader, pastor, teacher, overseer, and spiritual father.

Pastor Dell has been happily married to his wife, Jill, for over thirty-seven years. They have two sons, one daughter, and four grandchildren. They reside in Valdosta, Georgia.

www.ingramcontent.com/pod-product-compliance
Lightning Source LLC
Chambersburg PA
CBHW072007090426
42740CB00011B/2122